Language Essentials for Teachers of R

Module 9

Teaching Beginning Spelling and Writing (K–3)

Second Edition

Louisa C. Moats, Ed.D.

Presenter's Kit by Carol Tolman, Ed.D.

7 8 9 10   B&B   19 18 17

ISBN 13: 978-1-60218-996-6
ISBN 10: 1-60218-996-X
JDE #: 178343/07-17

Printed in the United States of America
Published and distributed by

4093 Specialty Place • Longmont, Colorado 80504 • (303) 651-2829
www.soprislearning.com

CREDITS
Cover, Zoe Houseman. © Adam & Imthiaz Photography.

How does copyright pertain to LETRS® Module 9?

Dedication

To my husband, Steve Mitchell, whose unwavering support makes LETRS possible.

—LCM

Acknowledgments

LETRS® modules have been developed with the help of many people. The National LETRS Trainers, who currently include Carol Tolman, Mary Dahlgren, Nancy Hennessy, Susan Hall, Deb Glaser, Judi Dodson, Pat Sekel, Anthony Fierro, Danielle Thompson, and Anne Whitney, have all offered valuable suggestions for improving module content and structure. Carol Tolman has been an invaluable partner in the development of the presenter's materials and revision of the modules. Nancy Hennessy tactfully coaches me in ways to improve the content of LETRS.

Linda Farrell, Bruce Rosow, Kevin Feldman, Susan Lowell, Patricia Mathes, Marianne Steverson, Lynn Kuhn, Jan Hasbrouck, Marsha Berger, Susan Smartt, and Nancy Eberhardt all contributed their expertise to the first edition of LETRS. Many other professionals from all over the country who have attended institutes and offered constructive criticism and ideas have enabled the continual improvement of LETRS and related materials. I hope you see your influence on the revised editions.

I am grateful for the competent support of the Sopris editorial and production staff who have groomed this product for publication: Sharon Pendergast, Karen Butler, and Rob Carson. Special thanks are due to Toni Backstrom, who manages the LETRS program with enthusiasm, competence, and flair, and to Steve Mitchell, the publisher of LETRS.

—LCM

About the Author

Louisa C. Moats, Ed.D., is a nationally recognized authority on reading instruction, how children learn to read, why many people have trouble reading, and treatment of reading problems. Louisa has been a neuropsychology technician, teacher, graduate school instructor, licensed psychologist, researcher, consultant, conference speaker, and author. She spent 15 years in private practice in Vermont, specializing in evaluation of and consultation with individuals of all ages who experienced difficulty with reading, spelling, writing, and oral language. After advising the California Reading Initiative for one year, Louisa was site director of the NICHD Early Interventions Project in Washington, D.C., a four-year project that included daily work with inner-city teachers and children. Recently, she has devoted herself to the improvement of teacher training and professional development, leading the development and implementation of LETRS®.

Louisa earned her bachelor's degree at Wellesley College, her master's degree at Peabody College of Vanderbilt, and her doctorate in reading and human development from the Harvard Graduate School of Education. She was licensed to teach in three states before undertaking her doctoral work. In addition to LETRS, Louisa has authored and coauthored books including *Speech to Print: Language Essentials for Teachers*; *Spelling: Development, Disability, and Instruction*; *Straight Talk About Reading* (with Susan Hall); *Parenting a Struggling Reader* (with Susan Hall); and *Basic Facts About Dyslexia and Other Reading Problems* (with Karen Dakin). Instructional materials include *Spellography* (with Bruce Rosow) and *Spelling by Pattern* (with Ellen Javernick and Betty Hooper).

Louisa's many journal articles, book chapters, and policy papers include the American Federation of Teachers' *Teaching Reading Is Rocket Science*. Most recently, she contributed to the development of the Common Core State Standards in English Language Arts for the National Governors Association and Council of Chief State School Officers.

Contents

Chapter 3   Sentences

Chapter 4 **Supporting the Planning Process**

Chapter 5 **Enabling Translation**

Chapter 6 Review, Revision, and Publication

Introduction to LETRS®

LETRS® (*Language Essentials for Teachers of Reading and Spelling*) is professional development for educators who are responsible for improving K–12 instruction in reading, writing, and spelling. The content of LETRS is delivered in a series of 12 core modules in book format. Each module in the series focuses on one topic, with the topics aligned to be delivered in sequential training. Thus, one book for use in the course of training—and later as a professional reference—is provided for each module. Each module is typically delivered in a one- to two-day presentation by a national, regional, or local district trainer who has met the LETRS trainer certification guidelines developed by Dr. Moats and her colleagues.

> **module [mŏjūl] n.**
> a self-contained component of a whole that is used in conjunction with, and has a well-defined connection to, the other components

LETRS modules are used for both in-service training and for undergraduate and graduate courses in reading and literacy instruction. They can also be resources for any educator charged with improving the language skills of students. LETRS is designed so that participants will understand:

1. *How* children learn to read and *why* some children have difficulty with this aspect of literacy;
2. *What* must be taught during reading and spelling lessons and *how to teach* most effectively;
3. *Why* all components of reading instruction are necessary and *how* they are related;
4. *How to interpret* individual differences in student achievement; and
5. *How to explain* the form and structure of English.

LETRS modules are designed to be delivered in sequence, but flexible sequencing is possible. In sequence, the modules build on overview concepts and introductory content, and then on phonology, phoneme awareness, and the writing system (orthography) of English (Modules 1–3). Next, the modules progress to topics in vocabulary, fluency, and comprehension instruction (Modules 4–6). Later modules (7–9) target reading instruction for the primary grades and include this module on teaching spelling and writing. The final series (Modules 10–12), designed for educators who work with students at grade 3 and above, addresses advanced phonics and word study, comprehension and study skills in content-area reading, and assessment of older students.

A presenter CD-ROM (developed by Dr. Carol Tolman) accompanies each LETRS module, providing a PowerPoint® presentation that supports, extends, and elaborates on module content. The presentation slides are designed to be used by professional development personnel, higher education faculty, consultants, reading specialists, and coaches who have a strong background in the concepts and who have been trained and certified to present LETRS.

LETRS is not a reading instruction program, and LETRS modules do not substitute for program-specific training. Rather, LETRS complements and supports the implementation of programs aligned with scientifically based reading research (SBRR). A complete approach to improving reading instruction must include: (a) selection and use of core and supplemental instructional materials; (b) professional development on how to use the materials; (c) professional development that leads to broader understandings; (d) classroom coaching and in-school supports; (e) an assessment program for data-based problem-solving; and (f) strong leadership. A comprehensive, systematic approach with these elements will support a Response to Intervention (RtI) initiative.

We recommend that teachers who have had little experience with or exposure to the science of reading and research-based practices begin with LETRS *Foundations* (Glaser & Moats, 2008). *Foundations* is a stepping stone into the regular LETRS modules. Other related resources have been developed to support LETRS professional development, including:

- LETRS Interactive CD-ROMs for Modules 2, 3, 4, 7, and 8 (developed with a grant from the Small Business Innovation Research [SBIR] program of the National Institute of Child Health and Human Development [NICHD]), which provide additional content and skill practice for topics often considered challenging to implement and teach in the classroom.
- *ParaReading: A Training Guide for Tutors* (Glaser, 2005)
- *The Reading Coach* (Hasbrouck & Denton, 2005)
- *Teaching English Learners: A Supplementary* LETRS *Module for Instructional Leaders* (Argüelles, Baker, & Moats, 2010)
- LETRS *for Early Childhood Educators* (Paulson & Moats, 2009)
- *Teaching Reading Essentials* (Moats & Farrell, 2007), a series of video demonstrations used extensively by LETRS trainers throughout the delivery of training.
- LETRS Online, which encompasses three online professional development courses based on LETRS. Now available from Cambium Learning® Sopris, each online course is equivalent to a three-credit-hour class; the courses may be taken for credit if requested.

LETRS *Foundations of Reading Instruction*

Foundations of Reading Instruction offers educators the opportunity to access approximately 18 hours of instruction online. This course includes video lectures by Dr. Louisa Moats and national LETRS trainer Dr. Deborah Glaser; online exercises and activities; and links to recommended resources, relevant research, and online text from LETRS *Foundations*. Specific topics include oral language, vocabulary, comprehension, phonemic awareness, phonics, fluency, assessment, progress monitoring, and effective teaching recipes.

LETRS Modules 1–3: Literacy Instruction: Phonology, Phonics, and Spelling

The course teaches how children learn to read; explains why some struggle and fail; and develops an understanding of phonemic awareness, phonics and word study, and spelling. It provides more than 30 hours of online course content based on video lectures by national LETRS trainer Dr. Carol Tolman and LETRS creator Dr. Louisa C. Moats, video modeling of instruction, online exercises and activities, links to recommended resources, relevant research, and excerpts from the LETRS Interactive CD-ROM series.

LETRS Modules 4–6: Literacy Instruction: Vocabulary, Comprehension, and Fluency

The course focuses on the knowledge required for effective instruction in vocabulary, fluency, and reading comprehension. It emphasizes the interconnectivity of all elements of reading instruction and provides more than 30 hours of video lectures by LETRS creator Louisa C. Moats, video modeling of instruction, online exercises and activities, links to recommended resources, relevant research, and excerpts from the LETRS Interactive CD-ROM series.

The chart below represents a fundamental idea in LETRS—that language systems underlie reading and writing, and students' difficulties with reading and writing are most effectively addressed if the students are taught the structures and functions of language directly. We ask teachers to learn the terminology of language systems and to recognize that language is an important common denominator that links reading with writing, speaking, and listening comprehension.

Content of LETRS Modules Within the Language-Literacy Connection

Components of Comprehensive Reading Instruction	Organization of Language						
	Phonology	Morphology	Orthography	Semantics	Syntax	Discourse and Pragmatics	Etymology
Phonological Awareness	2	2					
Phonics, Spelling, and Word Study	3, 7	3, 7, 10	3, 7, 10				3, 10
Fluency	5	5	5	5	5		
Vocabulary	4	4	4	4	4		4
Text Comprehension		6		6	6	6, 11	
Written Expression			9, 11	9, 11	9, 11	9, 11	
Assessment	8, 12	8, 12	8, 12	8, 12	8, 12	8, 12	

Note: Numbers represent individual modules in the LETRS series.

Overview of Module 9

Writing instruction should be an integral part of reading and language arts instruction. Better writers are better readers; skills in both areas are dependent on the mastery of language. This module addresses the content and format of effective writing instruction for novices in grades K–3.

Beginning with an exploration of cognitive processes involved in writing, the module presents an integrated lesson framework grounded in research that combines skill development with process-oriented composition. The writing of sentences is examined in detail. Instructional techniques to support the three phases of the writing processes—planning, translating, and reviewing—are explored. The module includes the analysis of student writing samples, role-play of corrective feedback, and practical skills of lesson planning for better results.

Chapter 1 The Challenge of Learning to Write

Learner Objectives for Chapter 1

- Review national achievement data on writing.
- Identify the cognitive systems and processes that are engaged during writing.
- Distinguish the "lower-level" and "higher-level" language demands of writing.
- Understand the role of working memory in writing.
- Recognize, in student writing samples, which skills and processes appear to be underdeveloped.

Warm-Up: What Strategies Do You Use to Teach Writing?

Describe how you currently incorporate writing instruction and writing practice into your classroom instruction.

- How much class time do you spend on writing instruction/practice per day?

  Per week? _____

- In the context of what subject matter? _____

  _____

- What kinds of student groupings do you use? _____

  _____

- What program/materials/lesson frameworks do you use for guidance?_____

  _____

  _____

How Well Are Our Students Doing in Writing?

The most recent National Assessment of Educational Progress (2010) shows that we have made significant gains in early reading. Now only 33 percent of fourth-grade students score below the basic level and 34 percent are at the basic level, while 33 percent are either proficient or advanced in reading. This is an improvement; a decade ago, 38 percent of fourth-graders were below-basic in reading. The Reading First program of No Child Left Behind and the influence of the National Reading Panel (2000) can be credited for many of these gains (Foorman, Petscher, Lefsky, & Toste, 2010).

Far less attention has been paid to writing curriculum, instruction, and achievement than to reading, even though students who can write well do better on reading assessments (Jenkins, Johnson, & Hileman, 2004). The National Assessment of Writing, not surprisingly, shows that few students are masters of this craft. Eighth- through twelfth-graders take the National Assessment of Writing in conjunction with the National Assessment of Educational Progress. In 2002, only 2 percent of eighth-graders were deemed advanced, and 29 percent were proficient, in grade-level writing (Persky, Daane, & Jin, 2003). Sixty-nine percent were either at or below the basic level in writing. In 2007, eighth- and twelfth-graders made small gains in writing proficiency compared with 2002, but large gaps remain between the writing proficiency of white, middle-class students and students who are African-American, Hispanic, or Native American (National Assessment of Educational Progress, 2008). Girls score higher on the writing assessment than boys, and students from less-educated families and/or less-privileged socioeconomic backgrounds score lower than their more-privileged peers.

What are the implications of these statistics? For many students (and adults!), writing is difficult. It is more difficult than reading. We expect students with learning disabilities and dyslexia to struggle with writing, but they are not the only ones who face challenges. The majority of students need systematic practice, deliberate skill building, and many opportunities to write as they slowly develop proficiency over time. As with reading, writing comes easily and naturally to some students but is difficult for many others. This module is designed to explore why that is the case and to prepare teachers to use insightful and effective strategies in writing instruction for all students.

Why Writing Is Important

Exercise 1.1	List the Benefits of Writing

Take a few moments to list 10 ways in which writing enhances reading, understanding, academic performance, and life skills. Work with a partner on this exercise.

1. _____

2. _____

3. _____

4. _____

5. _____

6. _____

7. _____

8. _____

9. _____

10. _____

Writing is an essential skill for all students if they are to be successful in school and, eventually, in the workplace. Language arts classes directly assess students' written communication, but writing skills are valuable across a wide range of coursework. In social science, humanities, and science classes, writing well is indispensible for students to demonstrate knowledge and express ideas. Outside of the classroom, writing well is necessary to express oneself, persuade others, advocate a position, and accomplish many other tasks. It is also a skill that employers increasingly see as highly valuable in prospective employees (The National Commission on Writing for America's Families, Schools, and Colleges, 2004). Indeed, one study estimates that taxpayers across the United States spend $250 million annually on the extra training and oversight that are required to address writing deficiencies just among state government workers (The National Commission on Writing for America's Families, Schools, and Colleges, 2005).

Writing also benefits reading—at all levels. Reading comprehension is enhanced when students write a response to something they have read. Written responses record what students have learned. In generating a written response to reading, students must connect ideas, sort the important from unimportant, and pursue understanding. They must attend to detail and find support for ideas. At the word level, spelling or encoding language requires students to possess phonological awareness and attention to the details of print. Word choice during writing promotes vocabulary development. Mastery of sentence structure, metaphoric language, text organization, and narrative voice are more the product of writing than of reading. Students are naturally more intimate with language forms they have used in their own writing than they are with language they have encountered only during reading.

When students write about their experiences and ideas, they engage both personal and objective meanings at the deepest level. As writers, we talk with ourselves and to others about what we believe, and in so doing, discover much about what we know to be true.

Writing well brings tremendous benefits, but learning to write is a protracted and challenging process. Although writing has received less attention in research and public policy than has reading, several comprehensive overviews of writing research provide solid grounding for this module's theoretical frameworks and instructional approaches (Berninger & Wolf, 2009; Graham, MacArthur, & Fitzgerald, 2007; Troia, 2009). Valid theoretical frameworks help explain individual differences in writing development and guide the design of curriculum and instruction. Thanks to sophisticated cognitive research methods, we understand today, better than ever before, what is entailed within the act of writing and why so many students struggle.

Why Writing Is Difficult

The production of written language is the latest-developing, most challenging form of language use. Many adults with excellent reading comprehension are much less skilled at writing clearly. (Even some teachers are insecure about their writing abilities!) Likewise, many children who read well have difficulty learning to write. Among the language-dependent skills, writing takes the longest to learn and is mastered by the fewest.

The main reason why writing is difficult is that it is the quintessential mental juggling act. The act of composing, transcribing, and editing written language draws on all the processing systems needed for reading, as well as many others. Writing calls on numerous subskills, cognitive abilities, self-management strategies, memory functions, and attention resources. A writer's brain not only uses the four processors critical for word recognition (phonological, orthographic, meaning, and context), but also draws heavily on other language, motor, memory, attention, and executive functions.

Preparation for writing begins long before children reach kindergarten. Language foundations developed early in life include receptive and expressive language. Children must acquire a vocabulary and background information, knowledge of word use, a sense of standard syntax or sentence structure, and the ability to organize and produce verbal responses that are appropriate for a given context (Paulson & Moats, 2009). They also must gain enough life experience and social maturity to have ideas about a topic. Motor and sensory skills must be strong enough to support coordination of writing implements for letter formation. Working memory must develop enough for students to hold ideas in mind, in order to analyze how to put thoughts into written words, sentences, and paragraphs.

The mental demands of writing are obviously complex and varied, as represented in *Figure 1.1*. Let's explore the components of this model, one section at a time, and the role that each plays in writer development.

Figure 1.1 Cognitive Systems in Writing Production

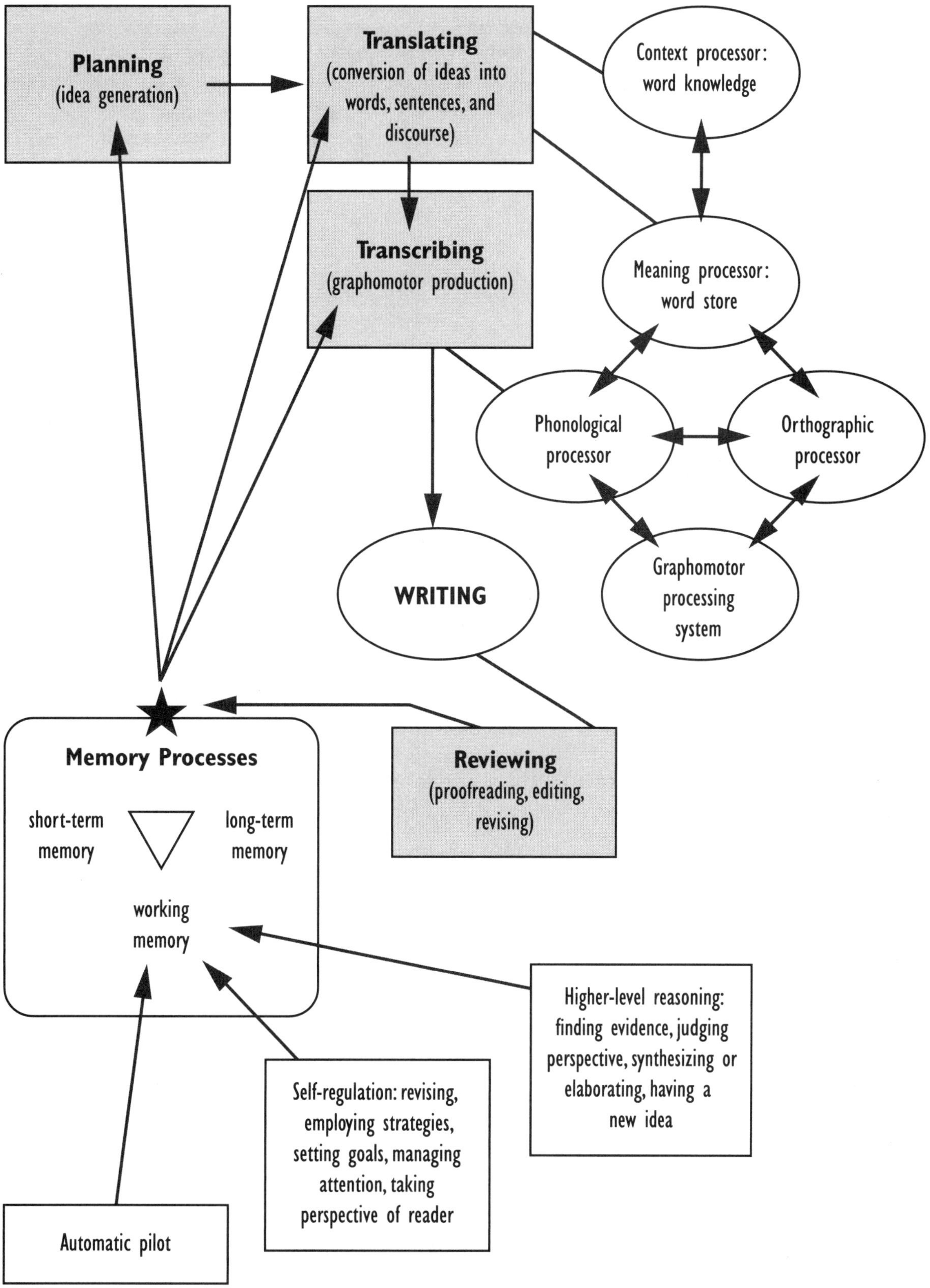

The Four (Plus) Language-Processing Systems

At the top right of *Figure 1.1* (previous page) is the schematic diagram of the four-part processing system involved in word recognition and spelling. As we explored in earlier LETRS® modules, each of the processing systems must play its part in order for a person to accurately and fluently recognize printed words and recall those words for spelling. To review:

The *phonological processor* perceives, stores, recalls, and mentally manipulates the speech sounds in spoken words. It is responsible for the development of phoneme awareness. If a student is aware of the phonemes that words comprise, those phonemes become "parking spots," or mental slots to which letters and letter patterns are mapped. Inner speech representations, residing in the phonological processor, are activated during reading and spelling, even if the person is not speaking out loud.

The *orthographic processor* perceives, stores, recalls, and mentally arranges the letters in written words. It is activated during printed word recognition and spelling. The more advanced a person's reading skills, the more heavily the brain relies on orthographic processing. Nevertheless, speech codes are activated during fast silent reading and automatic writing. Spelling recall requires communication between the orthographic and phonological processors, even when word recall is automatic.

The *meaning processor* is the repository for word meanings. Once a printed word is decoded or named, the meaning processor kicks in and tells us what the decoded word means. For spelling and writing, the writer links the intended meaning with the phonological and orthographic processing systems to recall the spelling of each word. In addition, during writing, the writer searches the mental lexicon or meaning processor for the words needed to express ideas.

The *context processor* is used in spelling to resolve which homophone to use (their, there, they're) or to select the right form of a word for the context of a particular sentence. For example, I must choose between the words sacks and sax for the sentence "I brought two _____ home after shopping." In addition, the context processor holds our knowledge of sentence structure, allowable word order, and the organizational structures of connected text (discourse).

Because we have been focused on reading in previous modules, we have not yet focused on *graphomotor* processes and their role in literacy. The term *graphomotor* comprises two Greek combining forms: *graph*, having to do with written language, and *motor*, having to do with coordination of movement. The term *graphomotor* refers to the skill of manually forming, on the page, letters that represent language. Graphomotor skill is necessary for controlling the direction, spatial proportion, flow, and size of letters during writing. The graphomotor processing system is wired into the language processors as soon as students know what alphabetic letters represent and begin to practice writing words (Berninger & Richards, 2002).

Before we move to consideration of the other cognitive systems at work during writing, let's compare two writing samples—one from a kindergarten student, the other from a first-grade student—to identify what we can understand about the students' phonological, orthographic, and graphomotor development based on their writing.

Exercise 1.2	Compare Kindergarten and First-Grade Writing Samples

Examine the two writing samples on pages 12–13, then complete the comparison chart with notes or phrases.

Question	Kindergarten Student	First-Grade Student
Has the student automatized standard letter formation?		
Does the student need more work on the use of uppercase and lowercase letters?		
Does the student have control over spaces and the alignment of writing on the page?		
Does the student represent the sounds in words (demonstrating grade-appropriate phoneme awareness)?		
Does the student have grade-appropriate command of high-frequency irregular word spellings (orthographic memory)?		
Does the student use punctuation appropriately (orthographic and syntactic knowledge)?		
Do you think the student was positively engaged by the task?		

(continued)

Exercise 1.2 (continued)

Kindergarten Student:

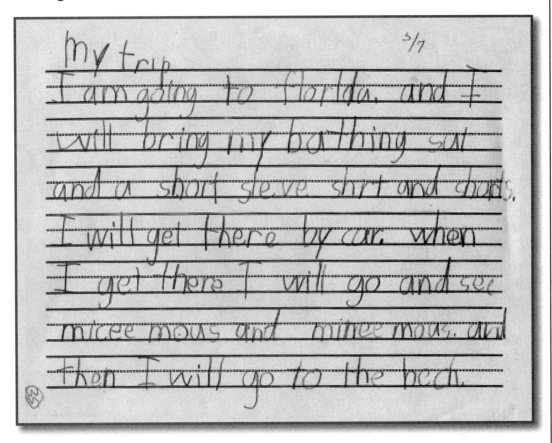

Translation: "My Trip. I am going to Florida, and I will bring my bathing suit and a short-sleeved shirt and shorts. I will get there by car. When I get there, I will go and see Mickey Mouse and Minnie Mouse. And then I will go to the beach."

Exercise 1.2   (continued)

First-Grade Student:

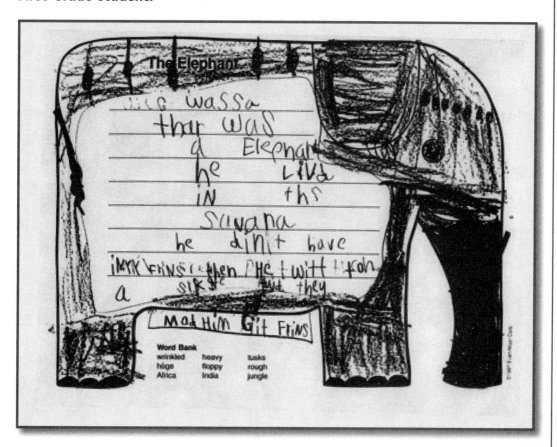

Translation: Once was a / there was / a elephant. / He lived / in the / savanna. / He didn't have / any friends. Then he went to / a circus, and they / made him get friends.

Now, write a short paragraph (three to five sentences) that compares these two students' development of phonological, orthographic, and graphomotor skills in relation to the overall quality of their compositions.

_____

_____

_____

_____

_____

_____

_____

A Three-Part View of the Writing Process

In *Figure 1.1* on page 9, the shaded boxes represent the primary components of the writing process, the steps the writer must complete to formulate and produce written language that conveys intended meanings. About 30 years ago, Hayes and Flower (1980) proposed a model of the writing process that heavily influenced writing education at the time. Keep in mind, however, that the Hayes and Flower conceptual model of writing was derived from self-reports of college students who verbalized their own thinking processes as they composed. Essentially, the model explains the mental activities of adult writers at the college level. Hayes and Flower maintained that there were three major sub-domains of written expression that worked recursively with one another during writing (see *Figure 1.2*). All processes could be active at any time: *planning* the writing, *translating* words into text, and *reviewing* and changing drafts. All three processes can be active at any time.

Figure 1.2 Three Recursive Mental Processes

| Planning | Translating Into Written Form | Reviewing and Revising |

Planning

The planning component of writing involves generating and organizing ideas. It should encompass the selection of a purpose for writing, decisions about the organizational structure the author will use, and audience identification. In the planning process, the writer also may have to draw on ideas prompted by a given stimulus, such as a text, a picture, or an experience. This is the part of writing in which we try to identify what it is that we have to say and how we are going to say it.

Translating

In the translating phase of the writing process, ideas are converted into specific words, and the words are transcribed into written form. Ideas from the planning phase may be reformulated, reorganized, or discarded during the generation of written text. The translation phase of writing requires syntactic formulation, which is the piecing together of sentences that convey intended meaning and that conform to conventional standards of spelling, punctuation, grammar, and usage.

Reviewing

In the reviewing phase of the writing process, the writer reviews, edits, and/or rewrites text. Reviewing can take place midstream; it does not always happen after completion of the first draft of text. Many writers edit continually as they translate words onto the page. Reviewing requires the writer to stand back and reflect on what he or she has generated, preferably from the point of view of the person(s) who will be reading the finished work. An effective reviewing phase also requires the writer to evaluate how the piece will be interpreted by the audience.

Hayes and Flower's portrait of the mental juggling act of writing has heavily influenced educational practice for many years. It has contributed to the view that writing instruction should emphasize activities such as brainstorming and generating ideas, producing a series of drafts, interacting with an intended audience to revise and improve the composition, and using publication as the motivation for editing.

The concern about writing instruction based on the Hayes and Flower model is that Hayes and Flower developed the model using self-reports of college students who verbalized their own thinking processes as they composed. Essentially, the model explains the mental activities of adult writers at the college level, for whom activities such as spelling, word recognition, and typing or handwriting are largely automatized. Teachers working with younger students must be cognizant that they are simultaneously learning both "higher-level" and "lower-level" writing skills, which can place exorbitant demands on their working memory and other cognitive functions.

"I try to write a little bit every day."

"Higher-Level" and "Lower-Level" Writing Tasks

Before we extend this discussion to the unique characteristics of young children learning to write, let's clarify what we mean by "higher-level" aspects of writing and "lower-level" aspects of writing. "Higher-level" sounds lofty and more valuable than "lower-level," but both are crucial in writing development and instruction. Let's make a simple comparison chart.

Exercise 1.3	List Higher-Level and Lower-Level Cognitive Demands

List what you consider to be some of the higher-level cognitive demands of writing and the lower-level skills necessary for accomplishing those higher-level tasks.

Higher-Level Cognitive Demands	Lower-Level Cognitive Skills
1. Using a story structure or expository structure.	1. Physically forming the letters using pencil on paper.
2.	2.
3.	3.
4.	4.
5.	5.
6.	6.
7.	7.
8.	8.

You may have noticed that our field likes to dichotomize the subcomponents of writing along the lines of what we consider higher-level and lower-level skills. Developers of writing tests like to use the word *mechanics* for handwriting, spelling, punctuation, and capitalization and the word *composition* for the process of putting together ideas. Some writing tests—such as that used by the National Assessment of Educational Progress—intentionally avoid scoring spelling, in order to keep the test a relatively "pure" assessment of composition skills. Even in the new Common Core State Standards, the "writing" section focuses entirely on higher-level composition. It does not address students' ability to form letters; spell; or use age-appropriate vocabulary, grammar, or writing conventions such as punctuation and capitalization (see *Appendix A*). The document's standards for mastery of spelling, word usage, and language structure are listed under a different section, called "language" (see *Appendix B*).

And yet, just as in reading, proficiency in writing requires mastery of both higher-level and lower-level skills. In reading theory, the "simple view" states that reading is the product of word decoding and comprehension. It is dependent on both lower- and higher-level language processes:

> **Word Decoding x Language Comprehension = PROFICIENT READING**

If students are weak in either component, then their reading development will be limited. The relationship between these components is known, and students' skills in each area can be measured. Only by considering both aspects of reading can we understand how to design and interpret assessments, and how to design and deliver instruction.

Figure 1.3 illustrates a similar "simple view" of writing, which is analogous to the reading model but adds the mental control processes that are so important to the mental juggling act of writing.

Figure 1.3 Simple View of Writing

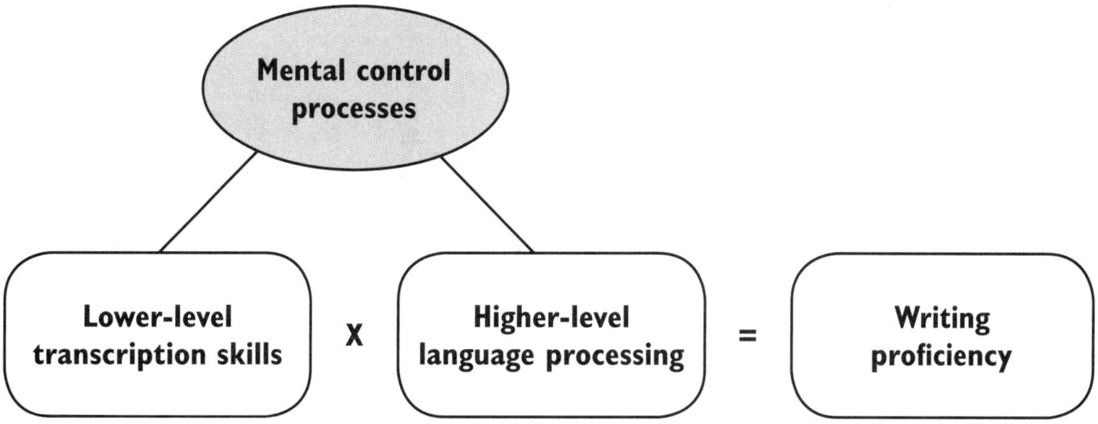

Some Differences Between Children and Adults

Young children's writing processes are significantly different from those of competent adults (Berninger & Richards, 2002; Berninger & Wolf, 2009) because they have not yet acquired the building blocks for production of written language. Unfortunately, advocates of the "writing process approach" tend to overlook the fact that developing writers are not like educated, mature adults. The Hayes and Flower studies were conducted on college students who had long ago automatized the "lower level" skills listed in *Appendix B*.

Berninger and others have used the Hayes and Flower model to prove that the *translating* component of writing—which encompasses the application of words to ideas and the manual transcription of those words—accounts for much of the variability in the competence of young children (Berninger, 1999; Berninger & Wolf, 2009). Whereas skilled writers already have learned how to put ideas into words and write them down, beginning writers must acquire many specific language-formulation and transcription skills at the same time they are learning to manage higher-level composition tasks. Failure to master the lower-level skills of writing limits what a young learner can accomplish at the higher levels, just as a decoding or fluency problem limits reading comprehension. And, as in reading, lower-level writing skills develop through incremental practice.

Many skills that are crucial to the writing process develop gradually and sequentially in the early grades. Early writing instruction can address the three major components of writing described by Hayes and Flower: planning, translating, and reviewing. To do so optimally, a curriculum must carefully orchestrate these components to emphasize essential skills in critical periods of development and to enable eventual integration of these skills in academic writing. Let's consider what young students' writing can tell us about their strengths and weaknesses.

Exercise 1.4	Evaluate Three Second-Grade Students

Three second-graders (none receiving special education services) were asked at the end of the academic year to write a description of how they would make breakfast for a friend. After a few minutes of discussion of the topic, they had 20 minutes to write. Look over the three writing samples, then answer each question that follows in complete sentences.

Exercise 1.4   (continued)

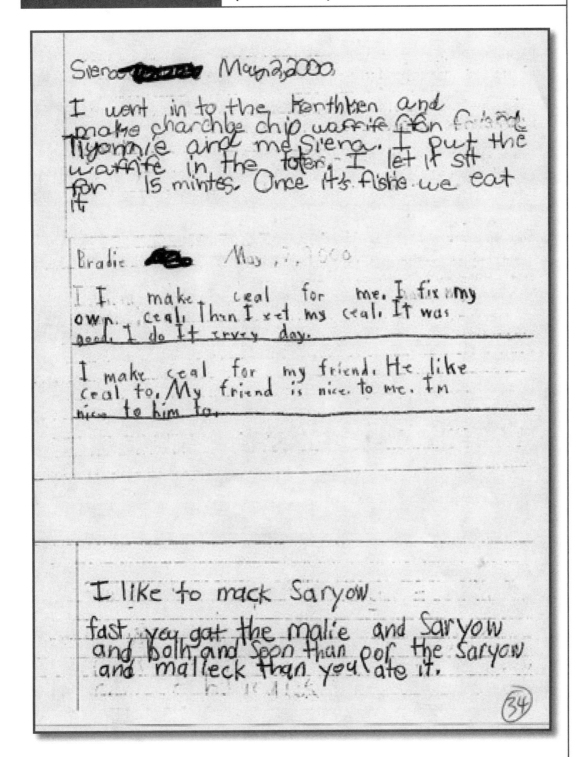

(continued)

Exercise 1.4   (continued)

Translations:

1. I went in to the kitchen and make chocolate chip waffles for Tyonnie and me, Siera. I put the waffle in the toaster. I let it sit for 15 minutes. Once it's finished, we eat it.

2. I make cereal for me. I fix my own cereal. Then I eat my cereal. It was good. I do it every day. I make cereal for my friend. He likes cereal, too. My friend is nice to me. I'm nice to him, too.

3. I like to make cereal. First, you get the milk and cereal and bowl and spoon, then pour the cereal and milk, then you eat it.

Questions:

1. Which two students exhibit the least accurate phonetic representations in their spelling? Citing specific errors, defend your opinion about which students need additional work on phonological awareness and basic phoneme-grapheme correspondence.

    _____

    _____

    _____

    _____

2. Why do you think the sentences are so short in writing sample #2?

    _____

    _____

    _____

    _____

3. What is your best guess about the nature, quality, and amount of writing instruction these students have received?

    _____

    _____

    _____

    _____

    _____

The Role of Memory in Writing

Look back at *Figure 1.1* on page 9. The third section of the model—memory—is very important in understanding why some young children struggle with writing. We first mentioned the role of memory in Module 6 of LETRS®, in our discussion of reading comprehension. We mentioned that working memory is a key variable in a reader's ability to integrate meanings within a text and between a text and information stored in long-term memory.

Writing places even heavier demands on various memory systems than reading does. Before we can understand the role of memory in writing, we need to review in more detail how memory is structured and what each memory system does (Baddeley, 2001; Berninger & Richards, 2002) (see *Figure 1.4*).

Figure 1.4 A Reader's Goal: Mental Model

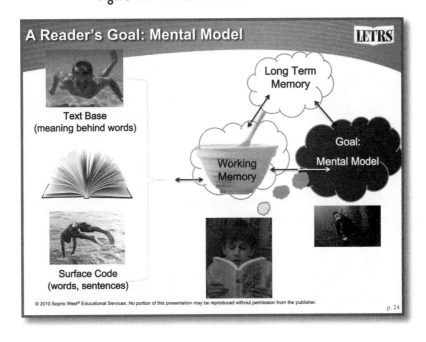

Three kinds of memory are depicted in the comprehensive model of writing: long-term memory, short-term memory, and working memory. *Long-term memory* is perhaps the easiest to describe. Long-term memory refers to the permanent mental storage of knowledge and impressions from experience, including information about the school we attended, a list of countries we have visited, and ideas we have learned about healthy living. We draw upon long-term memory when we connect incoming information with what we already know, or when we conjure up ideas and words to put down on paper.

Short-term memory, on the other hand, is a temporary storage system designed to record sensory and linguistic input for a few seconds—just long enough to make sense of it and decide whether to assign it to long-term memory. Short-term memory is passive and fleeting. For example, we are demonstrating short-term memory when someone tells us a new phone number. Most of us race to write down the number so that we will have a permanent record of it. Few of us can (or care to) remember all of the phone numbers we use.

Working memory operates on information in short-term memory, often integrating information held in short-term memory with long-term memories. Working memory is a very active memory system designed to hold onto and manipulate information during complex cognitive tasks. Baddeley (2001) portrays working memory as a multi-component system, as represented by *Figure 1.5.*

Figure 1.5 Model of Basic Working Memory Components

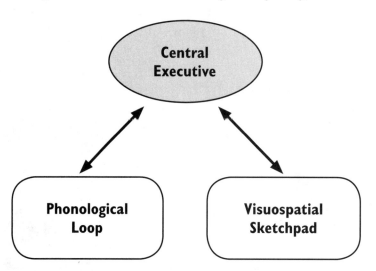

The visuospatial sketchpad and the phonological loop are storage components in the working memory system. The visuospatial sketchpad stores visual patterns, images, and spatial movement, while the phonological loop stores speech codes and verbal information. Like open filing bins full of temporarily stored information, these two components are acted upon by the central executive component. The central executive is the boss; it regulates, directs attention to, and manages the decisions that take place in working memory. The central executive also connects information across the two storage systems.

The familiar task of saying digit sequences backwards illustrates the activities of working memory. Repeating a series of numbers in reverse order requires much more mental work than listing the same numbers in forward sequence. To successfully repeat digits backwards, we may use one of several strategies: we may rehearse the names of the numbers; we may picture them in our minds while we name them; or we may try to use an association trick, such as matching part of the series to some other familiar idea. In this task, the central executive of our working memory may decide to engage the phonological loop (the names of the numbers); the visuospatial sketchpad (the images of the written numerals); or information in long-term memory that will aid recall.

Working memory plays a major role in all phases of writing (Vanderberg & Swanson, 2007). When we spell words, the central executive directs their production. While holding the speech sounds of a word or phrase in the phonological loop, the central executive selects from the visuospatial sketchpad the graphemes necessary to write the word, and directs the hand to write their shapes. These processes are automatic when we know words well, but consume more attention and working memory capacity when words are unfamiliar or difficult. If letter formation and spelling are not automatized, the writer expends available cognitive resources managing transcription instead of keeping track of the topic, the sentence, or the intended sequence of ideas.

During every phase of composition, self-regulation depends on working memory. As the writer plans the piece, he or she must hold onto ideas temporarily, select or reject them after reflection, and organize them for further development. Setting a goal, choosing a format, and imagining the finished product depend on active mental sorting of ideas. Once a plan is determined, every word, phrase, sentence, and paragraph that is written must be evaluated for its alignment with the goal and the plan; otherwise, cohesion is lost. Successful revision depends on constant evaluation of cohesion and clarity and the ability to change what is not working well. As words are read, rehearsed, replaced, or added, the phonological loop is heavily engaged. The central executive must rapidly but purposefully shift attention from one aspect of the task to another as the writer navigates a series of choices and rearranges words to suit his or her purpose.

Finally, working memory plays a role in the higher-level reasoning processes necessary for composition. Working memory supports mental activities such as finding evidence to bolster an assertion, judging whether the voice or perspective of the author is consistent, and synthesizing ideas across segments of text. Working memory integrates ideas held "on-line" with information stored in long-term memory. All of the processes and phases of written composition are facilitated by working memory.

For young writers who have not yet automatized letter formation or spelling, the limits of working memory are taxed by forming each word on the page. Some young students struggle simply to remember words long enough to write them down—even during dictation of a short sentence. Many others develop working memory capacity slowly, after much practice, and take years to coordinate the mental activities that underlie planning, translation, and revision.

Exercise 1.5 — Observe Working Memory at Work

Read the compositions of two additional second-grade students, who were also asked to write a description of how they would make breakfast for a friend. Then, discuss with a partner how the writing samples differ. What can "T." do that Jasmine has not yet mastered? Could memory processes play a role in these differences?

Jasmine ▓▓ May I, 2000

French Toast

1. first you take the french toats out the bag.
2. Then you git a plate, crup and forkan butternilt.
3. Then you put the french Toast in the toaster for 2 mins.
4. Then you git the french toast out the toaster.
5. The you put the french toast on the plate.
6. Then you cut the french toast in half.
7. Then you put the crup on the french toast.
8. Then you and a friend eat the breakfast.

Exercise 1.5   (continued)

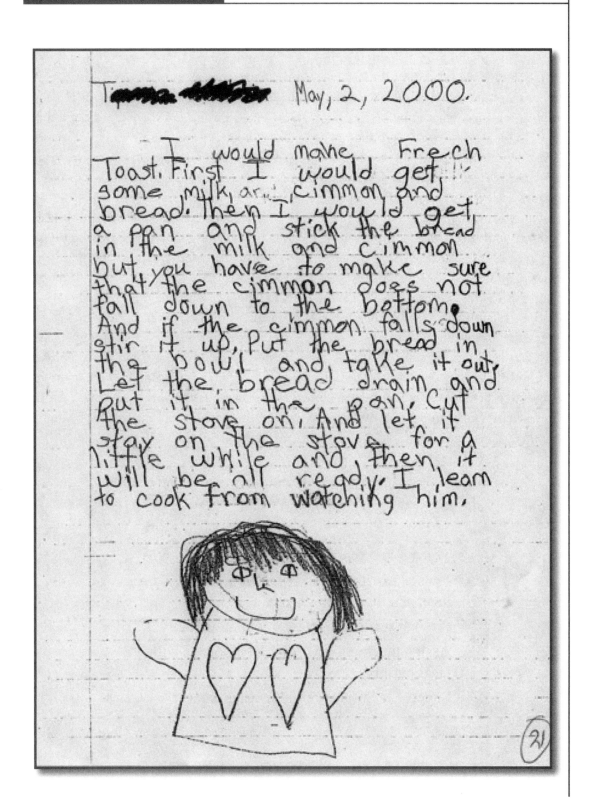

Tama ~~Miller~~   May, 2, 2000.

I would make Frech Toast. First I would get some milk, ar. cimmon and bread. Then I would get a pan and stick the bread in the milk and cimmon but you have to make sure that the cimmon does not fall down to the bottom. And if the cimmon falls down stir it up, Put the bread in the bowl and take it out, Let the bread drain and put it in the pan, Cut the stove on, And let it stay on the stove for a little while and then it will be all ready. I learn to cook from watching him.

Theory Into Practice: An Integrated Lesson Framework

In this chapter, we have sketched the major cognitive processes and mental activities involved in the mental juggling act of written expression. Given these models of how our minds work to produce a piece of writing, the challenges for a young writer should be obvious. Writing is a complex and demanding activity that entails selection of a purpose, the use of strategies for planning and organization, translation of ideas into conventionally written text, and the ability to monitor one's own production of text and then revise and improve it.

Working memory plays a major role in all aspects of writing, and when it is fully engaged in both lower-level and higher-level writing tasks, it can limit a student's writing capabilities. The lower-level writing skills—including letter formation, sentence-writing fluency, spelling, spacing, punctuation, and capitalization—demand a great deal of a student's available attention until those skills become automatic. Meanwhile, the higher-level writing skills—such as selecting words, forming sentences, and organizing ideas—are also placing heavy demands on the student's working memory.

As with reading, writing can be taught even to students who are not "natural" writers. Good instruction is systematic, direct, and purposeful. Young writers need assignments that are genuinely engaging and that provide guided opportunities to practice both higher-level and lower-level writing skills. Writing lessons in the primary grades should occur between three and five times per week, for about 30 minutes per lesson. Skill development and composition practice should both be included in the lesson framework (see *Table 1.1*). The next few chapters address the many ways to support this basic lesson framework, beginning with the foundational skills.

LETRS Theory Into Practice: Summary

- Teach 3 to 5 times/week for about 30 minutes
- Include instruction and practice in both lower level and higher level skills
- Provide sufficient practice for automaticity
- Assign meaningful writing assignments with a clear purpose
- Support each stage of the writing process

Table 1.1 Framework for Integrated Writing Lesson for Grades 1 and 2

5–10 Minute Warm-Up to Build Transcription Fluency

Includes student activities such as:

- Forming a few letters, using numbered arrow cues, tracing, verbalizing, or writing from memory, then evaluating accuracy.
- Producing the alphabet, in sequence, one or two times per session, until fluency is achieved.
- Writing graphemes for dictated phonemes (vowels and consonants), including letter combinations such as vowel teams and digraphs.
- Combining onsets and rimes to write whole syllables.
- Writing high-frequency words to dictation—a few at a time, singly, or in sentences—saying the letters while writing each word.

10–20 Minutes: Compose With Teacher Modeling and Assistance

Planning

- Establish the goal of the activity.
- Help students establish the topic; use prompts as appropriate.
- Build or elicit topic knowledge from students.
- Show or create a model of a finished product.
- Generate and list ideas for writing.
- Help students arrange ideas in order.
- Think, pair, share: Have students share with a friend before writing.

Drafting (translating ideas into words and translating words into writing)

- Compose in dialogue with the students, writing down what they say on a chart, overhead, or cue cards.
- Begin sentences with the students, and have them complete the sentences.
- Encourage students to prompt themselves with self-talk or partner-talk.

Reviewing and revising (as appropriate after conferences)

- Have students share writing with peers or adults.
- Talk over what can be added, deleted, elaborated, or rearranged.
- Lift one or two sentences from a student's work to demonstrate proofreading and editing.

Chapter 2 Teaching Handwriting and Spelling

Learner Objectives for Chapter 2
- Explain the relationships among handwriting, spelling, and composition.
- Define *dysgraphia*.
- Identify and practice the most powerful techniques for teaching letter formation.
- Review a progression and principles for spelling instruction.

Warm-Up: How Fluent Is Your Handwriting?
Work with a partner; exchange the roles of writer and timer. Time your partner writing the cursive alphabet with his or her non-dominant hand. Then time your partner writing the alphabet with his or her dominant hand.

Time for non-dominant hand: _____

Time for dominant hand: _____

Why Teach Handwriting?

The most common characteristic of poor or novice writing is its brevity and sparseness (Bain, Bailet, & Moats, 2001; Moats, Foorman, & Taylor, 2006). Young students often list ideas in an unconnected manner, without sufficient elaboration. Such sparse communication of ideas may indicate problems with vocabulary, grammar, spelling, punctuation, capitalization, and/or handwriting. Effective instruction builds these basic skills, while providing practice with purposeful, meaningful written communication.

Classrooms where a "writers' workshop" approach dominates the writing curriculum often neglect handwriting instruction (Troia, Lin, Monroe, & Cohen, 2009). Students may be left to figure out for themselves how to form the letters; the implied belief is that handwriting will happen naturally, through exposure, and that handwriting instruction is irrelevant to composition. However, research makes clear that the opposite is true: When students automatize correct letter formation early in writing development, their spelling and composition skills are likely to be stronger (Berninger & Wolf, 2009; Graham, 1999; Graham, Berninger, Abbott, Abbott, & Whitaker, 1997).

Both legible handwriting and fluent handwriting benefit composition in the early grades. The motor skills necessary for letter formation are considerable (Graham & Weintraub, 1996). They include sufficient muscle strength to hold the writing implement, fine motor control to direct the implement precisely, kinesthetic awareness of the intended movement, rhythmic flow of movement, and the ability to drag the hand steadily across the page. A sense of directionality is also important, because letter formation involves controlled production of a series of strokes in varying directions. Most young students can develop all these aspects of graphomotor control with frequent, distributed practice and explicit teaching.

Dysgraphia

The term *dysgraphia* refers to a specific learning disability that affects the production of handwriting. Indications of dysgraphia include illegible letter formation; absence of the graphomotor control necessary to write within lines; and slow, laborious production of written work. The difficulty with letter formation affects production of both uppercase and lowercase letters, as well as the overall arrangement of writing on the page.

Like other learning disabilities, dysgraphia may occur alone or in conjunction with other learning difficulties. Dysgraphia may affect individuals who are otherwise very intelligent and who are able to formulate ideas verbally. Individuals with dysgraphia usually are poor spellers as well. Many—but not all—are dyslexic, experiencing a specific reading disability related to weaknesses in phonological processing and word recognition. Boys are affected by dysgraphia more often than are girls; moreover, boys in general are slower to master the graphomotor skill of handwriting.

One word of caution related to diagnosing students with dysgraphia: A student who has not been taught how to write may appear to be dysgraphic until he or she receives appropriate instruction. Such an individual may respond very well to instruction (Wolf, 2005). Measurement of a student's response to instruction should be part of any diagnosis of a learning disability affecting writing.

Handwriting and Keyboarding

Is the computer making handwriting irrelevant? Should we simply teach keyboarding to students whose handwriting is difficult to read? For several reasons, keyboarding cannot, and should not, be a substitute for handwriting instruction, except for students who are severely dysgraphic and simply do not have the graphomotor coordination to learn to write.

First, navigating life is going to be difficult for anyone who cannot write answers to questions on exams, send notes to other people, address envelopes, create lists, complete government forms, and fill in job applications by hand. Second, writing words helps us remember them. The act of encoding with our hands improves retention of letter and word images in memory (Weiser, 2010). Third, even if a person can use a keyboard proficiently, he or she will likely be required to engage in written communication at times when a computer is not available. Finally, until students learn to type very well, they typically write more fluently—with more complex syntax and with better-formed ideas—when they write by hand than when they peck out words on a computer (Berninger & Wolf, 2009). For all these reasons, handwriting instruction should be a fixture in the writing curriculum beginning in kindergarten.

Students should also be taught keyboarding, beginning in first grade, if not before. However, do not encourage students to type out their compositions until they have developed sufficient typing speed and accuracy.

Establishing Accurate Graphomotor Memories

In order for correct letter formation to support fluent transcription, the brain must establish a motor memory linked to the orthographic processing system. The memory for a letter should be accessed without conscious attention. Therefore, it's important to establish letter formation habits early in a student's writing education. If students "invent" letters for very long, they establish habits—and not necessarily the ones we want them to have. Several days of practice working on a letter is preferable to practicing too many letters at once. The saying "perfect practice makes perfect" applies; modeling, practice, and corrective feedback are important from the beginning of handwriting instruction.

Exercise 2.1   Learn to Form a New Symbol

Look at the new symbol for /ă/ on the presenter's slide. Watch your presenter model the formation of the symbol. Use the verbal cues and numbered arrows to produce the symbol in this space:

_____

_____

_____

The goal of handwriting instruction is the development of graphomotor habits, or automatized sequences of pencil strokes for each letter, made in a specific direction, with size relative to other letters. Letter formation is automatic when the component strokes are executed accurately without conscious effort. Letter formation requires more than hand-eye coordination. Letters are codes for speech sounds; thus, the motor habits that enable letter formation are connected neurologically to the language centers of the brain. The brain receives sensory feedback from the hand and directs the timing and direction of letter production, but at the same time, letters are processed as symbols for speech. Therefore, recall is enhanced if students associate letter names with letter shapes and sounds.

Tips for Teaching Letter Formation

Berninger has conducted controlled experiments to compare methods for teaching letter formation (Berninger & Wolf, 2009). She has concluded that optimal instruction for young learners incorporates the following steps:

1. Teach lowercase manuscript first, then practice uppercase letters. Move to cursive in second or third grade.

2. Sequence the introduction of letters according to groups with similar basic strokes, such as those suggested in *Table 2.1*.

3. Use lined paper (with top, middle, and bottom lines in each row) that has well-marked margins. The top line can be the "hat line," the middle line the "belt line," and the bottom line the "foot line," as cued by a man figure sketched on the left margin. (This technique is used in *ReadWell*, a program developed by Marilyn Sprick for Sopris West.)

4. Check student posture, pencil grip, and paper position. Accommodate left-handed students by tilting the paper toward the left.

5. Name a letter, then demonstrate the letter's formation by verbally describing each stroke as you model writing the letter.

6. Supply a modeled letter that uses numbered arrows to remind students of the order and direction of strokes.

7. Ask students to imitate the motion with their whole arm, with index and middle fingers pointing, tracing in the air or on a rough surface.

8. Ask students to trace on top of a well-formed letter on paper before they cover up the model and write the letter from memory. Always have students name the letter as they write it.

9. Ask struggling students to trace over the model letter on a large surface, such as a chalkboard, before trying to write it between lines on paper.

Table 2.1   Groupings of Lowercase Manuscript Letters for Handwriting Instruction

The following suggestions for letter groupings in handwriting instruction represent one way to accomplish the goal of systematic instruction. Some very good programs integrate letter formation into letter-sound and/or letter-name instruction, using equally effective methods. Other suggested letter groupings and additional guidance about instruction can be found in Wolf (2005), Berninger & Wolf (2009), and materials published by the Slingerland Institute for Literacy (www.slingerland.org) and the Neuhaus Education Center (www.neuhaus.org).

	VERBAL CUES
Group 1: Continuous movement	
h	Hat line down, up to belt line, hump forward.
b	Hat line down, up to belt line, forward around.
m	Belt line down, hump, hump.
n	Belt line down, hump.
r	Belt line down, up and hook.
p	Belt line down, below foot line, up and around.
Group 2: Letters with continuous movement, beginning at 2 o'clock below belt line	
a	Curve up, back, around, then down.
c	Curve up, back, around, leave open.
d	Curve up, back, around, up, down.
g	Curve up, back, around, down below foot line, hook back.
o	Curve up, back, around, all the way.
q	Curve up, back, around, down below foot line, hook forward.
s	Curve up, back, around, slant forward, curve back.

(continued)

Group 3: Letters with straight down strokes	
i	Belt line down, dot.
l	Hat line down.
t	Hat line down, cross.
k	Hat line down, slant in, slant out.
f	Curve up to hat line, down, cross.
j	Belt line down below foot line, curve back, dot.
Group 4: Letters with slanted lines (diagonals) beginning at the belt line	
v	Slant down and forward, slant up and forward.
w	Slant down and up, down and up.
x	Slant down and forward; slant down and back.
y	Slant down and forward; slant back below the foot line.
Group 5: Letters with horizontal lines	
e	Straight across, back around, leave open.
z	Straight across, slant down and back, straight across.
Group 6: Letter with a scoop	
u	Down, scoop up, down.

Determining a Student's Hand Preference

About 8 to 10 percent of the population is left-handed. Left-handedness occurs somewhat more frequently in boys than in girls. However, people's hand preference is distributed on a continuum. Some people are fully ambidextrous, and some have mixed dominance (in other words, eye, hand, and foot preferences are not all on the same side).

To learn handwriting, students must establish dominance of one hand. Switching hands interferes with graphomotor habit formation because letter strokes move in a different direction with the left hand than with the right. To determine the preferred hand of a student who seems to be unsure, use one or more of these tests—without telling the student that you are looking for hand preference:

- Stand in front of the student. Hand the student a pencil in the middle of his or her body. See which hand the student uses to reach for the pencil.
- Ask the student to show you how he or she would throw a small ball. (Don't tell them that you are looking for hand preference!)
- Watch the student engage in other fine motor activities, such as cutting and pasting. Which hand does the student use more frequently?

Developing Handwriting Fluency

Measurable goals, based on research, can be referenced for alphabet writing and for sentence writing fluency (Beck, Conrad, & Anderson, 2009; Berninger & Richards, 2002). A fluent adult can produce the cursive alphabet in 20 to 30 seconds. A third-grader should be able to produce the manuscript alphabet in well under a minute. Once students can copy connected text accurately from a model, fluency should improve with writing practice. Be sure to emphasize and reward accuracy and legibility before emphasizing writing fluency.

Berninger and her colleagues have published multiple studies (see Berninger & Wolf, 2009) showing that brief fluency drills benefit writing just as fluency drills benefit reading. Brief fluency-building exercises support students' ability to focus on the higher-level demands of composition by developing the lower-level skills until they are accurate and automatic.

The ideal framework for a writing lesson that culminates in composition includes warm-ups—exercises for the hand and the mind that are analogous to the warm-up drills players practice before a basketball or baseball game. For 5 to 10 minutes, students practice the basics: letter formation, alphabet production, sentence copying, word spellings, and sentence completion. Drills are brief, frequent, and varied, and when they are juxtaposed with writing process instruction, they are more likely to generalize to, and have a positive effect on, composition.

How Spelling Supports Writing

Like automatized handwriting, accurate and automatic spelling supports fluent writing. Spelling requires more specific word knowledge than reading does. To spell a word, we must know all the letters, whereas we can read a word if we recognize only part of the letter sequence. Spelling depends on knowledge of word structure at three distinct levels: sounds, syllables, and morphemes. To learn spelling, a student must pay close attention to the internal detail of spoken and written words.

When students are writing, if they expend mental energy wondering how to spell common words that are central to their compositions, that task will consume much of their available cognitive "desk space," so they will have little attention to pay to the higher-level demands of composition. For this reason, spelling and overall writing proficiency are highly correlated in third- and fourth-graders (Abbot, Berninger, & Fayol, 2010; Moats, Foorman, & Taylor, 2006). Better spellers are better writers.

Exercise 2.2 | Take a Quick Spelling Test

Now your presenter will dictate three words for you to spell here:

_____

_____

_____

When the test is over, reflect on why you might have had trouble spelling one or more of these words accurately.

Principles of Spelling Instruction

In kindergarten and first grade, spelling and reading can be taught using the same words. After first grade, spelling instruction must be treated as a separate enterprise; students should be able to read many more words than they can spell, so the same word lists and word study lessons are appropriate for only the best spellers. In second and third grades, many students require separate spelling instruction, in addition to the writing lesson, in order to master complex word structures, including the following:

- Complex consonant patterns (e.g., -**ch** and -**tch**, soft-**c**, and -**ck**)
- Two- and three-consonant blends (**qu**, **str**, **squ**, **spr**, **thr**)
- Vowel-Consonant-**e** spellings for long vowels (**ate**, **ode**, **use**, -**ive**)
- Vowel team spellings (**ee**, **ea**; **ai**, **ay**; **igh**; **oa**, **ow**, **oe**; **ue**; **ou**; **oi**, **oy**)
- Jobs of letter y to spell vowels (**cry**, **baby**, **gym**)
- Vowel-**r** spellings (-**er**, -**ur**, -**ir**, -**ar**, -**or**)
- Inflections (-**s**, -**es**, -**ed**, -**ing**, -**er**, -**est**)
- The Doubling Rule (**win** → **winning**; **hop** → **hopped**)
- The Drop Silent-**e** Rule (**hope** → **hoped**; **slime** → **slimy**)
- The Y-Change Rule (**study** → **studied**; **baby** → **babies**)
- Common homophones (**two**, **to**, **too**; **fare**, **fair**)
- The most common prefixes and derivational suffixes (**un-**, **re-**, **dis-**; -**ment**, -**less**, -**ful**)

Following are eight research-based practices that a spelling instruction program should incorporate (see Joshi, Treiman, Carreker, & Moats, 2008-2009; Moats, 1995):

1. *Frequent, distributed practice.* Throughout the week, a variety of brief exercises should engage students in writing the lesson's words many times.

2. *Word lists that illustrate a spelling pattern. Table 2.2* includes suggestions for the scope and sequence of spelling instruction, by grade level.

3. *Tasks that require careful analysis of both speech and print.* Students should be asked to think about and identify word structure, including phoneme-grapheme correspondence, syllables, and morphemes.

4. *Introduction of three to five irregular words each week.* Some of the highest-frequency words needed for writing are irregular "heart" words. Students can analyze these words by sound so that they explicitly identify the irregular part. *Table 2.3* on page 39, lists high-frequency irregular words, and *Table 2.4,* also on page 39, summarizes a method for teaching them.

5. *Explanation of syllable types and syllabication.* Students should "chunk" longer words systematically.

6. *Use of words in meaningful contexts.* Cloze sentences, sentence dictations, and writing a theme-based story with the lesson's words can provide contextualized practice.

7. *Word sorting for pattern recognition.* Sorting words provides hands-on, engaging opportunities to discover patterns. (See *Table 2.5,* page 40.)

8. *Proofreading practice.* Proofreading tasks promote better self-monitoring during writing.

Appendix C illustrates these practices in a sample spelling lesson from *Spelling by Pattern, Level 2* (Hooper & Moats, 2010).

Table 2.2 Spelling Scope and Sequence for Grades 1–3

	Grade 1	**Grade 2**	**Grade 3**
Beginning consonant sounds	**b-, d-, f-, g-, h-, j-, c-, k-, l-, m-, n-, p-, qu-, r-, s-, t-, v-, w-, y-, z-**	**ce-, ci-, cy- = /s/; ge-, gi-, gy- = /j/**	
Ending consonant sounds	**-b, -d, -g, -l, -m, -n, -p, -r, -t, -x; -s, -z = /z/; -ve = /v/**	**-ff, -ll, -ss, -zz** (floss rule); **-ge, -dge**	
Digraphs	**sh, th, ch, wh, ng, -ck**	**-ch, -tch**	**ph, gh = /f/**
Beginning blends	consonant + /l/ or /r/; **sk-, st-, sl-, sm-, sn-, sp-, sw-**	**shr-, thr-, scr-, squ-, spl-, spr-, str-**	
Ending blends	**-mp, -st, -nd, -nk, -ft, -lt, -lf**	**-cks = /x/**	
Silent letters		**kn, gn, wr, lk**	**s(t), -bt, -mn**

(continued)

	Grade 1	Grade 2	Grade 3
Short vowels (closed syllables)	a, e, i, o, u		
Vowel teams and diphthongs	ee, ea, oa, ai, ay	igh; au, aw; oi, oy; ou, ow; oo	eu, ew, ue, ui; eight, ough, aigh
Open syllables (single long vowels)	e, o y = /ĭ/	a, e, i, o, u y = /ē/	y = /ī/
Vowel-Consonant-**e** (VCe)	a_e, i_e, o_e, u_e, e_e	consolidate pattern	ore, are, ure, ire, ere
Vowel-**r**	er, ar, or (non-variant)	-ir, -ur, -er = /er/; -oar, -air, -ear; war, wor	er = /ar/
Rime chunks	-ing, -ang, -ung; -ink, -ank, -unk; -all		
Inflections and ending rules	plural -s = /s/, /z/; -ing, -en	-ed = /t/, /d/, /ed/; -er, -est (no base change); Doubling Rule, Drop Silent-**e** Rule	Y-Change Rule, Doubling Rule, and Drop Silent-**e** Rule; multisyllabic words
Prefixes		un-, re-, mis-	dis-, in-, ex-, con-, com-, per-
Derivational suffixes	-y, -ish, -able	-less, -ness, -ful, -ly, -ment	-tion, -ive, -age, -ic, -ity, -ible
Base words, roots	compound words	contractions; base words whose forms do not change when endings are added	multisyllabic Anglo-Saxon base words

Table 2.3 High-Frequency Irregular Words

the	were	many	door
a	there	been	their
have	they	what	often
of	are	where	very
off	says	some	would
one	said	come	could
only	again	from	should
do	you	other	friend
to	your	through	walk
two	want	put	talk
does	who	push	love
was	any	pull	gone

Table 2.4 Steps for Teaching an Irregular Spelling Word

1. Explain why some words are irregular. Many of the most common words in English are from old Anglo-Saxon. Words were pronounced differently hundreds of years ago, but their spellings may have stayed the same. Thus, the spelling and the sounds no longer match.

2. Say the word; ask students to say the word.

3. Segment the sounds with manipulatives, and map the graphemes to the phonemes.

4. Identify the parts of the word that are irregular or unexpected.

5. Trace a model, naming the letters as you write them.

6. Trace the model several more times, if necessary, then have students copy it three times.

7. Ask students to create a mental picture of the word.

8. Cover up the letters, and have students write the word from memory.

9. Check their writing immediately, and correct if necessary.

10. Monitor retention. If a student writes the word from memory three days in a row, you can put the word in the "learned" word bank.

Table 2.5 Example of a Versatile Word Sort

Have students sort words in one of four ways:

1. By spelling of /ō/,

2. By presence or absence of inflectional suffixes,

3. By number of syllables, or

4. In alphabetical order.

flowed	throng	elbow
yellow	throw	toad
snowed	toasted	broke
owner	throat	road
coach	window	soap
coast	soaked	floating
shadow	growth	boasts
croak	know	quote

From Hooper & Moats, *Spelling by Pattern, Level 2,* Lesson 12.

Exercise 2.3 | Identify Spelling Errors in Students' Writing

The following sentences were lifted from second-graders' written work. Each sentence contains one or more misspelled words. Can you identify a specific spelling concept that each student needs to learn?

1. I'm *gowing* to make breakfast for my friend.

2. I will put it on a *plaet* (**plate**).

3. I will sit *donw* and eat.

4. I will cook *pancake.*

5. *Frist, yous* (**use**) eggs.

6. I'm going to have a *chawBaer* (**strawberry**).

7. We made *froot silit* (**fruit salad**). You need *grabes* and *strawberrys* and *watermelem.*

8. You can make pancakes with *agg* and with *mike* (**egg** and **milk**).

9. I like to make *breakthis.*

10. Then the *yok* (**yolk**) comes out of the egg.

11. I *craked* it; then the slime came out.

Integrating Handwriting and Spelling Into Writing Instruction

Handwriting and spelling are foundational skills for writing. Both disciplines deserve daily, direct instruction in the classroom until students master their fundamentals. Methods for instruction in handwriting link visual cues (numbered arrows, lines, and models) with verbal cues in support of letter formation. Students who have learned to form the letters correctly and to manage the directional, fine motor, and spatial requirements of handwriting are likely to write compositions that are more substantive, better organized, and longer. As with reading, when students automatize lower-level writing skills, cognitive "desk space" is freed up for higher-level thinking about purpose, organization, audience, wording, and images.

Instructors must approach spelling as word study or language study, not rote visual memorization of unrelated words. Analyzing words helps students remember them. Effective spelling instruction calls attention to the sound structure of language, orthographic patterns and regularities, and the syllable and morpheme structures of words. It also puts modern spelling in the context of word origin (etymology). Almost any word can be explained from one of these angles.

Finally, students must use their knowledge of spelling in meaningful writing assignments. They need to know why spelling skills are important, just as they would understand the purpose of practice in a sports environment or a music lesson. Thus, the best instructional format for writing juxtaposes warm-ups of the underlying spelling and handwriting skills with opportunities for writing about engaging topics.

"I hope you realize that I'm the one who has to write about this stupid vacation next fall."

Chapter 3

Sentences

Learner Objectives for Chapter 3

- Define *sentence*.
- Review grammatical roles of words and parts of speech.
- Distinguish between phrases and clauses.
- Sort phrases, independent clauses, and dependent clauses.
- Define and identify simple, compound, and complex sentence types.
- Explore implicit and explicit methods of teaching sentence sense to young writers.

Warm-Up: Define *Sentence*

What is your definition of a sentence?

A Sentence Is ...

A sentence is a group of words that express a complete thought—but what is a complete thought? Is there another way to define *sentence*? More precisely, a sentence is an abstract linguistic frame that has slots for categories of words and phrases (see Moats, 2010, for a deeper discussion of linguistic categories and phrase structures). Certain slots must be filled in order for a sentence to be complete. Other slots are optional. A basic sentence must have a subject (the something that the sentence is about) and a predicate (which describes what the subject does, feels, or is). The subject must be a noun or noun phrase; the predicate must include a verb or verb phrase. Therefore, a simple sentence is a noun phrase plus a verb phrase:

$$S = NP + VP$$

The sentence structure and the words filling the sentence's slots all carry meaning. Word meanings often depend on the role the word plays in a sentence, and sentences, of course, must have meaningful words to make sense. The meaning of the word **port**, for example, depends on its sentence context. Compare "We sailed into **port**" with "The men drank **port** after dinner" with "That is a **port**able canoe." Many words in English can fill different slots in a sentence frame. In order to be understood, however, a speaker or writer must comply with the word order and usage conventions that others will understand. The underlying structure of a sentence permits only certain kinds of words in certain slots. Still, the number of words that can fit in each slot is vast, which allows for endless creativity in sentence generation. Thus, sentence production is both creative and constrained by shared norms.

Although every adult speaker knows—at least subconsciously—the rules and conventions for sentence production, effective writers must take their understanding of sentences a step further. Clearly expressing ideas through writing depends very much on the conscious manipulation of words within sentence structures. Experts do not agree on the best ways to teach grammar, syntactic awareness, or sentence production (Graham & Perin, 2007), yet students must gain command of these skills before they can write effectively. A strong composition depends on strong sentences.

Good writers know how to think about word order and its relationship with the ideas they are trying to express (Scott, 2004). Good writers can examine a sentence that seems awkward, incomplete, poorly phrased, or ambiguous, then resolve the problem through conscious correction of the sentence's faults. In order to edit in this way, a writer must be able to dissect and manipulate a sentence, which means the writer must have a linguistic toolbox at his or her disposal. The fine art of sentence crafting develops over a long time with frequent practice, just like any other competence.

The Roles of Words in Sentences (Parts of Speech)

Why should we bother teaching students about the traditional parts of speech? Traditional labels enable us to think about words in relation to their function in a sentence frame. Labeling the parts of speech allows us to identify and question what role a word is playing (e.g., "That's an adjective, and what you need here is an adverb!"). It enables us to discuss whether the sentence's required roles are filled (e.g., "You need a verb in this sentence."). And it gives us a framework for talking about whether a sentence has too much of a good thing (e.g., "Can you use a more precise noun instead of a string of adjectives?").

Moreover, a word's part of speech affects its spelling—for example, **course** is a noun, whereas **coarse** is an adjective. A word's suffix may determine its part of speech; therefore, the suffix might also provide information about the word's spelling and meaning (e.g., **practical** has the adjective suffix -**al**, while **particle** has no suffix and is a noun).

Exercise 3.1	Brush Up on Labels for Word Functions

Below is a short passage. Can you identify the role that each word is playing in the sentence frame? Label the role of each word, using the code in *Table 3.1*, page 46.

    c art adj

Then the Yellow Corn-Maiden brought from under her torn blanket a pouch, [which was]

made of buckskin and artfully beaded with turquoise and the whitest shells.

—Adapted from Tony Hillerman. (1972). *The boy who made dragonfly.*
Albuquerque, NM: University of New Mexico Press.

Distinguishing Types of Phrases

A *phrase* is a natural grouping of words that work together to fill a slot within a sentence frame. *Noun phrases*, *verb phrases*, and *prepositional phrases* are the three main categories of phrases, although adjective and adverbial phrases exist as well. Each phrase type contains words in that grammatical category. A noun phrase must contain a noun, a verb phrase must contain a verb, and a prepositional phrase begins with a preposition. The sentence "The toy soldier danced wildly to the music" includes a noun phrase (**the toy soldier**), a verb phrase (**danced wildly**) and a prepositional phrase (**to the music**).

Every sentence must have a subject containing a noun or noun phrase and a predicate containing a verb or verb phrase (see *Figure 3.1*, page 47). Additional words in the sentence can elaborate on, or modify, these basic sentence parts, but those additional words must fit within the basic sentence structure of subject and predicate. The subject can contain one or more noun phrases that include a determiner and optional adjective(s); the predicate can contain direct and/or indirect objects and adverbs, adverbial phrases, or prepositional phrases, in addition to the verb phrase.

Table 3.1 Traditional Parts of Speech

Part of Speech	Meaning Expressed	Examples
Noun (N)	Person, place, thing, or idea; name for something concrete or abstract	preacher, valley, antique, belief, consideration
Pronoun (PN)	A word or phrase that substitutes for a noun	I, me, you, she, he, they, that, its
Noun marker—article or determiner (Det)	Word that precedes or marks a noun	a, an, the
Verb (V)	Word for an action, state of being, or occurrence	twist, know, inundate
Verb to be as the copula (Cop)	Main verb linking the subject to the subject complement in a verb phrase	am, are, is, was, were, be, being, been
Auxiliary verb or helping verb (Aux)	A verb joined with the main verb to give more information about tense, mood, number, voice, or person	be, have, do, are, has, will, does, should, would, could
Adverb (Adv)	Modifies (tells more about) a verb, adjective, or adverb; a describing word	well, poorly, persistently
Adjective (Adj)	Modifies a noun; a describing word	rosy, outrageous, festive
Preposition (Prep)	Shows the relationship of one thing to another	against, in, under, on, around, beside, over, of, above
Conjunction (C)	Joins words, phrases, or clauses to one another	and, although, but, or, yet, then

Figure 3.1   Basic Sentence Structure

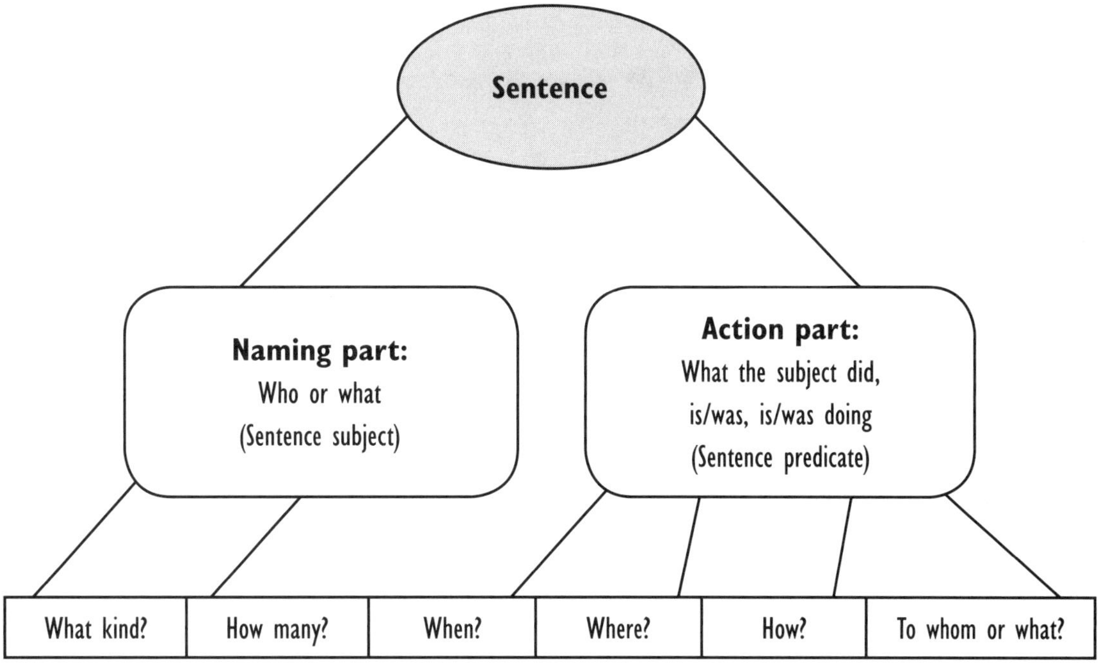

```
                        ┌─────────────┐
                        │  Sentence   │
                        └─────────────┘
            ┌───────────────┐         ┌──────────────────┐
            │ Naming part:  │         │  Action part:    │
            │ Who or what   │         │ What the subject did, │
            │(Sentence subject)│      │ is/was, is/was doing │
            │               │         │ (Sentence predicate) │
            └───────────────┘         └──────────────────┘
```

| What kind? | How many? | When? | Where? | How? | To whom or what? |

The verb controls the sentence. Which verb a predicate contains dictates which other slots the predicate must include. Some verbs must be followed by a direct object (e.g., "Sally spent **her mother's money**."). Other verbs are followed by a direct object and an indirect object (e.g., "Sally gave the **Red Cross** her **money**."). Some verbs take a direct object and a prepositional phrase (e.g., "Sally sent a **present to her cousin**."). Still other verbs take an infinitive (e.g., "Sally intended **to give** a present to her cousin."). Verbs are "marked" linguistically; if we know the features of a verb, we know what other words accompany it within the predicate.

Prepositional phrases tend to answer the *where, when,* and *how* questions. Prepositional phrases almost always contain a noun phrase after the preposition, which is why ending a sentence with a preposition seems odd (e.g., "Do you remember whom she came **with**?").

Here is a list of some of the most common prepositions:

aboard	concerning	past
about	considering	per
above	despite	plus
across	down	regarding
after	during	save
against	except	since
along	following	than
amid	for	through
among	from	to
anti	in	toward
around	inside	under
as	into	underneath
at	like	unlike
before	minus	until
behind	near	up
below	of	upon
beneath	off	versus
beside	on	via
besides	onto	with
between	opposite	within
beyond	outside	without
by	over	

Exercise 3.2 | Classify Types of Phrases

Next to each phrase, note which of three syntactic categories the phrase belongs to: noun phrase (NP), verb phrase (VP), or prepositional phrase (PP).

after the concert _____   the bitter cold winter _____   fluctuated daily _____

sold reluctantly _____   any golden variety _____   fed regularly _____

without a thought _____   over the top _____   deep knowledge _____

a chance encounter _____   was trekking _____   under the table _____

Identifying Types of Clauses

A *clause* is more than a phrase; a clause is a group of words that contains both a subject and a predicate. There are two kinds of clauses in English sentences: the *independent clause* and the *dependent clause*. An independent clause can stand alone as a sentence. A *simple sentence* is one independent clause. Here are some examples of independent clauses that stand alone as simple sentences:

- The teacher demanded her class's attention.
- She stood her ground.
- The class quickly complied.

A *dependent clause* also contains a subject and predicate; however, it cannot stand alone as a sentence. A dependent clause leans on, attaches to, and/or depends on an independent clause. It just doesn't sound right on its own. If a dependent clause is not attached to an independent clause, it is called a *sentence fragment*—an incomplete sentence. Examples of dependent clauses include:

- because they were overexcited
- while they settled down
- although it was a struggle at first
- when I was very young

Dependent clauses can be introduced by adverbial conjunctions, or *marker words*. There are many marker words that can signal relationships between sentences or between ideas within sentences. Some of them are:

> after, although, as, as if, because, before, even if, even though, if, in order to, since, though, unless, until, whatever, when, whenever, whether, while

Clauses can have compound subjects, as in:
- The **teacher** and the **principal** cooperated on discipline.
- The **boys** and the **girls** learned the rules.

Clauses can also have *compound predicates* with more than one main verb:
- Mrs. Smith **worked** long hours, **volunteered** for committees, and **taught** summer school.
- Each small group **read** the story, **discussed** its main characters, and **wrote** a response.

Exercise 3.3 — Differentiate Between Phrases and Clauses

Sort the following phrases and clauses into the appropriate column in the chart.
- whenever we go camping
- Perry called
- we dined out last Friday
- before twilight
- the tangled roots
- where Italian is spoken
- spectacular fine dining
- driven to distraction
- because he loves chocolate waffles
- after the performance ended
- the symphony concluded
- visiting can be tiresome

Phrase	Independent Clause	Dependent Clause

Simple, Compound, and Complex Sentences

A simple sentence is a single independent clause with a subject and predicate. A *compound sentence*, however, includes two or more independent clauses of equal importance. Independent clauses in a compound sentence are frequently joined by a coordinating conjunction. The *coordinating conjunctions* are *for*, *and*, *nor*, *but*, *or*, *yet*, and *so* (acronym: FANBOYS). These are compound sentences:

- I hesitated to yell, **for** I knew that my voice was tired.
- I advised him of his rights, **and** I defended him in court.
- They sought to follow the trail, **but** it was covered with thick brush.
- She said she wanted to save money, **yet** she went to the mall every weekend.
- We will get the petition signed, **or** we will not be able to register the candidate.

An *independent marker word* is a connecting word used at the beginning of an independent clause. Some common independent markers are: *also*, *consequently*, *furthermore*, *however*, *moreover*, *nevertheless*, and *therefore*. These words can begin a sentence that stands alone, but more often they connect parts of a compound sentence. When the second independent clause in a compound sentence begins with an independent marker word, a semicolon is needed before the independent marker word. For example:

- Sonja expected to finish the ski race; **however**, the race was cancelled before she had a chance to compete.
- Marjorie adores her new apartment; **nevertheless**, she is traveling much longer distances to work.
- Harold took the review class before his final exam; **consequently**, he aced the test.
- Teachers work hard; **therefore**, their pay should be increased.
- Students get credit for online courses; **moreover**, the online courses are less expensive than traditional courses.

A *complex sentence* is a sentence in which one or more dependent clauses are attached to or embedded in an independent clause. Complex sentences may introduce a dependent clause with a subordinating conjunction or a marker word, as in the following:

- **When** I was a novice, I got through every day on a prayer.
- **Although** she followed the new recipe, the cake didn't quite come out.
- **While** the dog wasn't looking, the squirrel escaped up the tree.
- **Until** she learned how to putt, Marnie refused invitations to golf.

Here is a partial list of subordinating conjunctions that can introduce a dependent clause:

> after, although, as, because, before, even, if, even though, in order that,
> once, provided that, rather than, since, so, than, that, though, unless,
> until, when, whenever, where, whereas, wherever, whether, while, why

Complex sentences may also include *relative clauses*, which are clauses that are introduced by a *relative pronoun*: *that, which, whichever, who, whoever, whom, whose, whosoever,* or *whomever.* For example:

- Charlie knew **that** the game was won.
- Mildred selected the larger oranges, **which** were grown in South America.
- Celine preferred people **who** let their needs be known.
- Please select **whomever** you prefer.

Exercise 3.4	Identify Simple, Compound, and Complex Sentences

Write "**S**" for simple, "**CP**" for compound, or "**CX**" for complex next to each sentence below.

_____ She was an old woman who lived at the bottom of the hill.

_____ The Incas built a city high in the Andes.

_____ The skin of poisonous frogs keeps predators away because it tastes bitter.

_____ Winter days are short, so we play more indoor sports in that season.

_____ Egyptian mummies were buried inside the pyramids.

_____ The dog barked incessantly, but the owners did nothing to stop it.

_____ Whenever the control tower gives the signal, the plane takes off.

_____ Carlos, the forward, sank the winning basket in overtime.

_____ The odds were in her favor, yet she still placed second.

_____ Whenever we are available, he is willing to guide us.

This very brief review of grammar and sentence structure has prepared us to shift our attention to writing instruction. We can now focus on some critical questions: What expectations are reasonable for developing writers? What is the best way to build sentence sense in young students? And can we outline an incremental, cumulative approach? The remainder of this chapter addresses these important questions.

What to Expect From Developing Writers

Normally developing children typically know the distinguishing features of orthography by the age of 2 or 3. Even at that young age, they know that writing differs from drawing in that it conveys a message, it is produced in a direction across the page (in English), it has distinct letter forms, and it can be read back. By age 5, the average native English-speaker has an intuitive or unconscious knowledge of all the basic sentence patterns in English and knows the meaning of perhaps 4,000 to 6,000 words.

By the beginning of kindergarten (age 5), students typically know some letter names, understand that spaces go between words, and recognize that writing runs from left to right and that print is organized from top to bottom on a page. Some students at this age attempt to write messages of their own and read them back. In addition, some kindergartners know the alphabetic principle—that letters of the alphabet represent the speech sounds in words—and can produce early phonetic spellings that represent some of the salient sounds in a word.

By the end of kindergarten, students should be either early phonetic or later phonetic writers (Ehri & Snowling, 2004). They should be able to form letters after being taught the motor patterns. They should spell by sound, using letter names and literal phonetic transcriptions of what they hear and feel as they say a word. They should also be able to correctly write a few high-frequency irregular words.

In kindergarten, students should begin to write words in sequence, with spaces between words and periods at the end of sentences. They may intuitively understand that sentences can "sound right" or "sound wrong," but they may think of a written sentence as nothing more than a group of words with a capital letter at the beginning and a period at the end. However, kindergartners' reading comprehension should enable them to answer basic questions, such as *who, what, where, when, why,* and *how,* and elaborate on sentences orally when prompted.

During first grade, students should become aware that a sentence has an underlying structure. They should know that sentences must have a subject (in other words, they must be about a person, place, thing, action, or idea) and that they must also have a predicate that tells about the subject.

By second grade, students should have enough mastery of basic transcription skills that they can attend to sentence composition and linkages between sentences. Students in second grade may be somewhat amenable to revision of their writing, especially in response to conferences with peers and adults. Second-graders should also start to adjust their approach to writing in accordance with the requirements of the task—in other words, depending on whether the assignment is a story, an explanation, an opinion piece, a poem, or a description. Teachers should expect second-graders to begin demonstrating greater independence in composition planning and idea generation. Linking sentences together in a basic paragraph should be a goal for students at this stage. *Table 3.2* (next page) summarizes reasonable expectations by grade level.

Table 3.2 Expectations for Young Writers' Development

Language Level	K–1	2	3
Words	• Achieves phonetic spelling of short, pattern-based words • Forms letters accurately • Knows 100 high-frequency words by the end of grade 1	• Maintains consistent letter spacing • Fluently forms letters • Exhibits transitional stage or conventional spelling, using regular short and long vowels	• Spells basic suffixes, vowel teams, vowel-r patterns • Knows how to write at least 300 high-frequency words
Phrases	• Uses basic noun and verb phrases	• Elaborates on a simple subject and predicate with adjectives and prepositional phrases	• Demonstrates flexibility in use of prepositional phrases and some adverbial clauses
Sentences	• Recognizes whether a sentence "sounds right" • Expands sentences orally when prompted • Answers questions with statements	• Writes in complete sentences with noun-verb-object structure • Combines two simple sentences into a compound sentence • Creates questions, statements, exclamations, and imperatives	• Produces complex sentences with sentence starters • Likely uses some sentence fragments and run-ons when writing • Begins to vary sentence patterns
Paragraphs	• Might indent without knowing why	• With support, links sentences in a basic paragraph structure (topic, details, conclusion)	• Writes two or three paragraphs together • Begins to use connectives and signal words that are appropriate for genre
Overall Cohesion	• May ramble in oral storytelling	• Stays on topic, although sentences may not flow well from one another	• Shows more control over topic, includes fewer extraneous details or comments, and more likely includes ideas in logical order

How to Build Sentence Sense

As early as kindergarten, students are expected to be able to formulate sentences, but those with language limitations do not understand at an abstract level what we mean by *sentence*. The definition of a sentence is more complex than "a group of words with a capital letter and a period." Sentences have a structure that is sensed but hidden, and they cannot be described or identified by surface characteristics such as the number or order of their words. Still, once students know how to think about sentence structure, they can fix an incomplete sentence, a run-on sentence, or a sentence that includes grammatical errors. The best approach to instruction is a combination of modeling, explanation, focused practice, and reinforcement.

There are many effective techniques for encouraging implicit and explicit awareness of sentence structure in younger students. Marking sentence parts, identifying the grammatical role of words, combining sentences, and expanding sentences systematically are among the techniques that early-grade instructors should use and practice. Judith Hochman, in *Teaching Basic Writing Skills: Strategies for Effective Expository Writing Instruction* (2009), offers a series of sentence-writing goals that provide a blueprint for instruction (see *Table 3.3*, next page).

Table 3.3 Sequence of Sentence-Writing Goals

TEACHING BASIC WRITING SKILLS

Student's Name: _____   Year: _____

Teacher's Name: _____   Grade: _____

Sentence Goals

	SEP.	JAN.	JUNE
1. Distinguish between a complete sentence and a sentence fragment.			
2. Convert a sentence fragment into a complete sentence.			
3. Identify a fragment(s) in a given paragraph.			
4. Rearrange sequences of words into a sentence, adding the correct punctuation and capitalization.			
5. Distinguish between a statement and a question.			
6. Write a statement with a capital letter at the beginning and a period at the end.			
7. Write a question with a capital letter at the beginning and a question mark at the end.			
8. Change a question to a statement and vice versa.			
9. Distinguish among statements, questions, exclamations, and commands, and punctuate each correctly.			
10. Write a statement, question, exclamation, and command about a given topic.			
11. Given a picture or text, write one or two questions about it.			
12. Write a question from a given response.			
13. Produce test questions for a unit of study.			
14. Write sentences using the conjunctions but, so, and because.			
15. Use subordinating conjunctions in the beginning or the middle of sentences.			
16. Combine two or more sentences.			
17. Produce complex sentences using sentence starters.			
18. Expand a sentence using two or three of the question words: *who, what, when, where, why, how.*			
19. Identify the question words (*who, what, when, where, why, how*) that were used to expand sentences.			
20. Identify the words in an expanded sentence that tell *who, what, when, where, why,* or *how.*			

I = Introduced   ✓ = Proficient

(continued)

Reprinted with permission from *Teaching Basic Writing Skills: Strategies for Effective Expository Writing Instruction* (Hochman, 2009).

TEACHING BASIC WRITING SKILLS

Sentence Goals

	SEP.	JAN.	JUNE
21. Use question words (*who, what, when, where, why, how*) to summarize the main idea of an article, event, picture, chapter, or story in one or two sentences.			
22. Identify and correct run-on sentences.			
23. Use correct end punctuation, commas, and capitalization.			
24. Identify subjects and predicates in sentences.			
25. Identify nouns in sentences.			
26. Distinguish between proper and common nouns.			
27. Identify action verbs in sentences.			
28. Identify adjectives in sentences.			
29. Add adjectives to sentences.			
30. Write sentences using adjectives.			
31. Identify pronouns in sentences.			
32. Substitute a pronoun for a noun and vice versa.			
33. Identify adverbs in sentences.			
34. Write sentences using adverbs.			
35. Identify an appositive (noun phrase) in a sentence.			
36. Write sentences using appositives (noun phrases).			
37. Identify nouns, verbs, pronouns, adjectives, adverbs, conjunctions, prepositions, and appositives.			
38. Correct number agreement in sentences.			
39. Correct tense agreement in sentences.			
40. Use varied and accurate vocabulary.			
41. Use internal punctuation correctly (commas, quotation marks, colons, and semicolons).			
42. Change a sentence from active to passive form and vice versa.			

I = Introduced   ✓ = Proficient

Listening for Sentence Completeness

Young students can begin sentence work orally and in shared writing activities. Start by providing a sentence fragment (either a subject or a predicate)—for example:

_____ ate the whole cake for dessert.

The barking dog _____.

_____ scared us in the darkness.

At recess, we _____ .

Then ask students, "What's missing? What is needed to complete the sentence?" You can fill in the blanks with the words that students produce.

Using a Sentence-Builder Chart

A sentence-builder chart describes the parts of sentences by the function of the words, rather than by the words' formal grammatical labels (see *Table 3.4*). This technique has been used traditionally by speech-language pathologists who work on syntactic development. Once students grasp the necessary and optional parts of a sentence, they can use the labels *nouns*, *verbs*, *adjectives*, and *adverbs* to replace the functional descriptions in the sentence-builder chart.

Table 3.4 Sample Sentence-Builder Chart

How many? Which ones? What kind of? (adjectives)	Who? What? (noun)	Is/was doing, feeling, thinking (verb)	To whom? To what? For whom? With what? (indirect object)	What? (noun phrase)	Where? When? How? Why? (prepositional or adverbial phrase)
The	baby	cried.			
The	baby	cried			loudly.
The laughing	baby	dropped		his toy.	
The sleepy	baby	put		his binky	into his mouth.
The hungry, tired	baby	screamed			with all his might when his mom left.
The friendly	baby	handed	me	his new toy	with both hands.

Practicing Sentence Expansion

Use sentence expansion to increase students' awareness of helpful details and precise descriptions. Have them expand simple sentences in response to the question words *who, what, when, why,* and *how,* in a series of small steps. For example:

1. Begin with a bare-bones sentence:
   The people ate cake.

2. Add one or more predicate expanders (*how? when? where?*):
   The people ate cake with their fingers at the birthday party last week.

3. Say more about the subject (*what kind? how many?*):
   The messy, happy people ate cake with their fingers at the birthday party last week.

4. Add detail; substitute stronger words.
   The messy, easy-going family gobbled cake using only their fingers at the wild birthday party last week.

You can also ask students to explore sentence expansion in reverse. Begin with a long, complex sentence and ask students to identify what words or word groups (phrases) answer the questions who, what, when, why, where, and how. For example:

who	*how*	*where*	*when*
The stealthy thief snooped quietly around the empty building early in the morning.			

Exploring Sentence Starters

Have students practice writing sentences using sentence starters that they would not normally choose. Identify a list of adverbial phrases or clauses that you would like them to learn to use to start sentences. Select a topic that the students are studying or reading about, and ask them to pick a few sentence starters from your list to say something about that familiar topic. For example:

Topic: **cave men**	Topic: **team sports**
In the prehistoric days, _____	Although our team is small, _____
Wherever they slept, _____	Even if the coach yells, _____
During a hunt, _____	Unless we get lucky, _____
Because they needed food, _____	Fortunately, _____
Against all odds, _____	

Sentence Coding, Using Colors

Color coding is used in the program *Multisensory Grammar and Composition*, by Dr. Suzanne Carreker of the Neuhaus Center in Houston. To start students on color-coding sentences, provide highlighters and explain that they should highlight:

- the subject of a sentence in yellow and
- the predicate in green.

Then they should circle:

- the subject describers with red and
- the predicate expanders with blue.

Sample sentences:

1. *Last year, our race team surprised everyone with a win.*
2. *The youngest student beat his older teammate.*
3. *At the finish line, we all cheered loudly.*
4. *Racing on a hot day can be tiring.*
5. *Some of us prefer friendly races with no prizes.*
6. *All six team members remember to drink water before we run.*
7. *Several girls surprised us with their speed.*
8. *Sometimes the volunteers take dogs on the walking path.*

Sentence Coding, Using Lines and Shapes

Lines and shapes are used by Victoria Greene and Mary Lee Enfield (2006) to teach sentence structure in Project Read's *Framing Your Thoughts*. This exercise models the technique but uses a different code. Where geometric shapes indicate sentence parts, have students label sentences following the pattern depicted in *Figure 3.2*.

Combining Sentences

Sentence combining has strong research support (Graham & Perin, 2007) as a method for improving sentence writing in students in grades 6 and up. Younger students can also benefit, as long as the teacher talks the class through the sentence manipulations and orally models how to combine the words.

1. Combine two simple sentences into a compound sentence, using pronoun substitution:
   - *Alice sat by the river. Alice saw a white rabbit run by.*
   - *Alice sat by the river, and she saw a white rabbit run by.*
2. Reduce a compound or complex sentence to multiple simple sentences:
   - *Alice, who was running after the white rabbit, followed him into the hole, after which she began falling down, down, down.*
   - *Alice was running after the white rabbit. She followed him into a hole. Soon after, she began falling down, down, down.*

Figure 3.2 Sentence Coding With Shapes

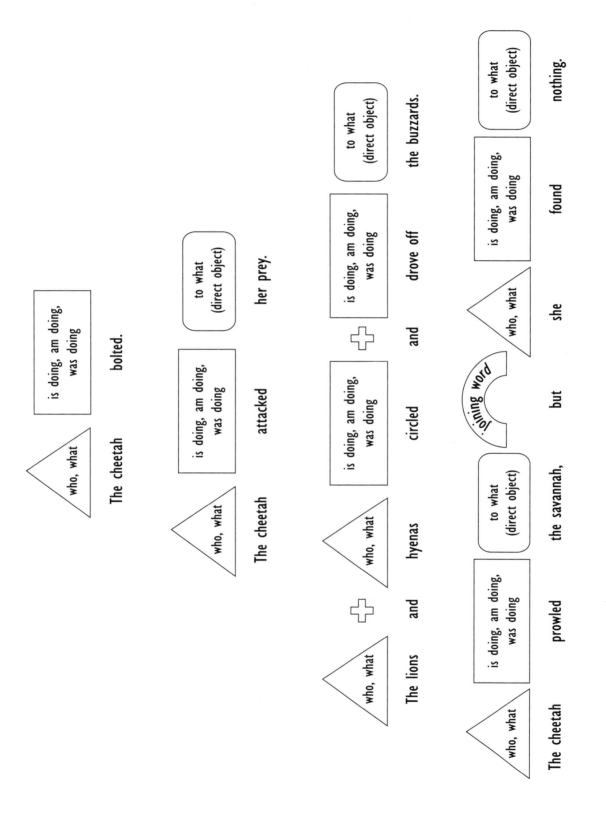

3. Combine two to four simple sentences into one complex sentence:
    *   *Alice noticed the cat. The cat was smiling. It was on the tree branch. The shadows were dark.*
    *   *Alice noticed the smiling cat on the tree branch, where the shadows were dark.*
4. Combine simple sentences into a compound or complex sentence, allowing for necessary changes in words:
    *   *The Mad Hatter smiled. He smiled at Alice. The Mad Hatter supposed that Alice was not telling the truth.*
    *   *The Mad Hatter leered at Alice, convinced that she was not telling the truth.*

Linking Clauses Using Conjunctions or Connecting Words

In order to write cohesive paragraphs, students must learn to link sentences using connecting words and references. Adult writers accomplish linkage by repeatedly referencing the topic, using pronouns, and using various kinds of signal and connecting words, among other devices. Specific vocabulary explicitly signals the relationships among ideas in different sentences.

Connecting words, or conjunctions, not only link thoughts together, but also capture the logical relationship between the ideas. Students gradually develop an understanding of these logical relationships (see *Table 3.5*). According to Jacobs (1997), children understand the concept of conjunctions (e.g., *and*, *both*) by second grade. However, most students do not fully understand disjunction between propositions or ideas (e.g., *but*; *either*, *or*) or use these words with logical consistency until sixth grade. Students continue to learn how to use statements of conditionality (*if*, *then*; *if and only if*) into grade 11.

In early stages of learning oral language, children show connection simply by proximity—that is, by saying sentences after one another. Next, they learn to use *and* for a number of meanings, including addition, time, cause, and condition. Then comes use of conditional terms such as *when*, *because*, *unless*, and *if*. Most children use conditional terms in oral language by the time they enter school. Mastery of these terms in writing, however, takes quite a few years.

Table 3.5 Progression of Children's Use of Conjunctions

First: Conjunction and sequence	Second: Causation	Third: Disjunction and alternation	Fourth: Conditionality
and both then when	because so	but or either, or neither, nor even though	unless although if if, then if only

Young learners' writing growth mimics their oral language growth. The first connective word that most children use for multiple purposes is *and*. Jacobs (1997) found that the repertoire for connective words among low-income second-graders included words for addition (*and*); time (*and, then, when*); and, to a lesser extent, causal relationships (*because, so*). Students a year older used words signaling disjunction (*but*) and the manner of action (*like, how*). Then, at and above grade 4, these students began using connecting words that express logical relationships, including alternation (*or*), general-to-specific (*for example*), and concession (*even though*). This study, then, suggests that students in early grades should benefit from:

- explicit instruction about words that connect ideas within and between sentences;
- practice using those words to connect simple sentences or elaborate on the ideas in sentences; and
- practice constructing compound and complex sentence forms that express cause and effect, conditionality, or subordination.

Diagramming Sentences

Traditional sentence diagramming may be too advanced a technique for primary-grade students, and opinions about its usefulness vary. Nevertheless, the technique can help teachers understand how to explain sentence structure. For an explanation of the classic Reed-Kellogg approach to diagramming sentences, see http://www.utexas.edu/courses/langling/e360k/handouts/diagrams/diagram_basics/basics.html.

Punctuation and Capitalization

Punctuation marks should be taught gradually, one convention at a time, to enhance the development of sentence composition skills. Each mark should be named, explained, then practiced in individual sentences. Having students highlight the marks in written passages and model the vocal expression signaled by the mark can also be effective in developing students' punctuation skills. On the next two pages, *Table 3.6* summarizes a general progression for punctuation instruction, and *Table 3.7* describes the order in which capitalization skills are usually taught.

Table 3.6 Sequence of Punctuation Instruction

1. **Period**
   - at the end of a statement
   - following a command
   - after an abbreviation
   - after numbers in a list
   - following an initial

2. **Question Mark**
   - after a question

3. **Comma**
   - in dates
   - in addresses
   - after introductory phrases or clauses
   - after the greeting of a friendly letter
   - after the closing of a friendly letter
   - between words in a list
   - to set off appositives
   - to separate a direct quotation from a sentence

4. **Underline**
   - underlining titles
   - underlining words used in a special way
   - underlining foreign words not commonly used in English

5. **Apostrophe**
   - before **s** in a possessive noun
   - in a contraction

6. **Exclamation Point**
   - at the end of an exclamation
   - after words showing strong emotion or surprise

7. **Dash**
   - to show a sudden break in a sentence
   - to emphasize a word, phrase, or clause
   - to indicate interrupted speech

8. **Colon**
   - between the hour and minutes in time of day
   - after the greeting in a business letter
   - before a long list

9. **Quotation Marks**
   - before and after the words of a speaker
   - around the title of a story, poem, or article

10. **Hyphen**
    - in some compound words
    - in compound numbers
    - marking syllable division at the end of a line

11. **Parentheses**
    - around words included in a sentence to explain or add information

Table 3.7 Sequence of Capitalization Instruction

1. A person's first name

2. A person's last name

3. The first word of a sentence

4. The word I

5. The date

6. Proper names for holidays and places

7. Names of streets and cities

8. Titles of compositions and books

9. Titles in names: Ms., Mrs., Mr., Dr.

10. Mother and Father when used as proper names

11. First word in the salutation of a letter

12. First word in the closing of a letter

13. Names of organizations and clubs

14. Names of states and other geographical locations

15. Commercial product names

16. First word of a quotation

17. Race and nationality

Practicing Sentences in Context

Clear, complete sentences supply the fabric for a strong composition. Kindergarten and first-grade students develop an early awareness of sentences through verbal modeling. One indication of sentence awareness is recognition of incomplete sentences. Gradually, through frequent and distributed practice, students build their competence at the sentence level and acquire an understanding of sentence parts. The list of sentence goals (Hochman, 2009) is a helpful guide for teachers, although students' acquisition of these skills is likely to be uneven and incremental.

Activities for sentence practice include color coding sentence parts, using a visual coding system to construct sentences, labeling the parts of a sentence by function, using sentence starters, and combining sentences. Most effective teaching strategies combine visual and verbal supports so that students can see a picture of the underlying sentence structures at work.

Sentence composition progresses much more smoothly if students are writing about topics they have studied, have experienced, or are learning about. Avoid writing assignments—even sentence-writing exercises—that occur in a contextual vacuum.

"My parents didn't write it—they just tweaked it."

Chapter 4 Supporting the Planning Process

Learner Objectives for Chapter 4
- Identify characteristics of an environment that motivates young writers.
- Explore three aspects of the planning process.
- Rehearse evaluation and selection of prompts.
- Examine a student writing sample.

Warm-Up: How Do You Motivate Students to Write?

Consider your own experience with young students who are asked to write their first compositions. What techniques or strategies have helped the students become motivated and focused on the task?

Creating the Right Setting

Students are more likely to write if the tools and prompts around them in the classroom environment create a setting that supports writing. It starts with materials. A writing center suitable for small groups can be stocked with simple equipment such as:
- pencils, colored pencils, markers, and highlighters;
- interesting photographs, paintings, or illustrations;
- lined paper of several kinds;
- letter-formation templates;
- materials for making book covers and binding pages;
- folders for individual student work, in a file box;
- display board for finished work;
- proofreading checklists;
- spelling dictionaries;
- children's magazines; and
- models or templates for a finished product.

The Planning Process

The planning process, the first of the three major components of composition, encompasses three distinct subprocesses:

- generating ideas,
- setting goals, and
- organizing and imagining the finished product.

Before diving into a composition, a beginning writer should have a plan or purpose for writing (a *goal*) and a plan for generating ideas (an *idea generator*). The writer must be motivated to communicate with an audience, whether it's real or imagined. Ideas can come either from fantasy or from prior learning and experience. During composition, the writer's thoughts must be *organized* in a way that draws on previous knowledge of text organization, strategies for crafting a piece, and/or the stated needs of the audience. Let's dissect how writers in the primary grades should approach each of these subprocesses.

Generating Topics and Ideas

When beginning writers sit down to write, they often wonder whether they have any ideas to express. While some young students are highly verbal and confident in their self-expression, others "draw a blank" and have difficulty formulating thoughts about a topic. Some causes for this "writer's block" include a limited vocabulary, limited life experience and background knowledge, limited knowledge of English, or limited ability with expressive language. Furthermore, students usually know that writing is not simply speech written down, and concerns about the inherent demands of the task may further inhibit their ability to express ideas.

A teacher working with novice writers should suggest topics for writing, for two reasons: first, to relieve less-verbal students from having to generate a topic; and second, to ensure that students practice different kinds of writing tasks. Most academic writing from fourth grade on will involve responding to reading, explaining the answer to a test question, writing a report, or expressing an opinion. Fantasy writing and unstructured writing do not prepare students for the demands of an intermediate or middle-grade classroom. Even early elementary students should begin tackling explanations, opinions, summaries, and comparisons as frequently as they write narratives.

Thus, many students will do better if, before writing begins, the teacher uses cues, supportive aids, or strategies such as the following:

- — Show a model of what is expected, or generate a model together with the class in "shared writing" (students talking, teacher writing) before asking individuals to compose on their own.
- — Think aloud about word selection while recording students' brainstorming ideas.
- — Read about a topic or share an experience organized around a topic.
- — Collect and post key vocabulary about the topic.

- Use visual prompts—such as photographs, paintings, sculpture, or curious objects—as springboards for discussion.
- Use the question words *who, what, where, when, how,* and *why* to help students elaborate on ideas.

Setting Goals

A student's goals for writing may be personal or audience-focused. Any writer is more likely to be invested in authentic goals when the assignment's purpose is clear. Personal goals should be negotiated between teacher and student, and should be explicit before writing is undertaken. Personal goals may involve the use of specific words or expression of specific ideas; correct application of specific writing skills, such as the use of transition words; or expression of feelings and thoughts that the writer wants to share.

When the goals are audience-focused, students benefit from a discussion about the needs and expectations of their intended reader(s). Will the piece be read by a friend? A pen pal? Parents? Another relative? Community members? What message does the writer need to communicate to this audience? What does the audience want to know?

Most primary-grade students benefit when a writing assignment requires them to write down an explicit statement of the goal or purpose for the assignment. Likewise, students generally benefit from use of self-monitoring strategies, such as remembering to ask oneself periodically who is going to read the writing, whether the words are on topic, and whether the writing is achieving its goal.

Organization

The organization of a piece of writing depends upon its purpose. Narrative structure is required if a student is writing about a real or imagined experience. Informative or explanatory text requires a different kind of logical structure designed to convey complex information or ideas. Arguments state opinions or make claims and support them with evidence. Lists, poems, letters, diaries, and memos have different structures as well. Young students who have read or been exposed to many examples of these various genres are better prepared to understand the distinctions among them.

The following instructional strategies are effective in building students' ability to effectively organize their thoughts in writing:
- Verbally rehearse how the piece will be organized, before writing begins;
- Show a model of the kind of writing that is requested, so that imitation or paraphrase of the model is possible; and
- Supply a visual organizational framework, such as a storyboard, semantic web, sequence chart, sentence starters, or outline of main idea and supporting details.

The Common Core State Standards (*Appendix A*) name three distinct genres of writing: argumentation or persuasion; informational or explanatory text; and narrative, which can be fiction or nonfiction, personal or imaginary. In kindergarten, students are expected to compose opinions, identify a topic and supply some information about their topic, and tell about a sequence of events. They are also expected to provide a reaction to that series of events. The Common Core State Standards expect students in first grade to be able to state an opinion and give a reason that supports their opinion. In an informational text, they should be able to not only state their topic, but also provide some facts in support of the statement and give the piece some sense of closure. A first-grader should write narratives that have two or more events in sequence, that use some signal words indicating sequence (e.g., *first*, *then*, *next*), and that provide a sense of closure. By second and third grades, students' ability to write opinion, informational, and narrative assignments should be more fully developed, and the students should tailor their use of vocabulary to each genre.

Descriptive writing can stand alone, or it can be embedded within the other three major genres. The Common Core State Standards does not specifically identify it as a genre, but descriptive writing can be taught independently of the other forms of writing. The following pages provide examples of organizational frameworks suitable for each genre and for teaching students in K–3.

Organizational Framework for Descriptive Writing

The goal of description is to evoke a visual image in the mind of the reader. The image can be of a person, place, thing, event, or abstract idea. Description requires the writer to supply detail describing the key attributes, characteristics, or behaviors of the subject, and to use words of space, movement, appearance, smell, taste, touch, or sound. Beginning writers can use the following frame to plan a descriptive writing project.

Planning Frame for Descriptive Writing

What words describe your person, place, object, or event?

Looks	Sounds	Smells	Tastes	Feels Like	Moves

Draw a Picture Here:

Organizational Framework for Narrative Writing

A narrative has a series of events that follow a progression and lead to a concluding event. Rather than providing a mere sequence of events, a compelling story revolves around a problem and the resolution of that problem. One or more characters contend with a problem between themselves and other characters; between themselves and nature or the world; or within themselves. Words that are often found in narrative texts include:

- first, second, third, next, then, last, finally
- eventually, previously, now, soon, before, after, when
- in the morning, toward evening, at nightfall, not long after, subsequently

Sequential Order Planning Frame

Tomorrow is my birthday, and we are going to have a special day. First, _____

_____ .

Next, _____ .

Then, _____ .

Finally, _____ .

Story Planning Frame

Setting (where, when)	
Characters (who, what)	
Problem (what must be solved)	

Event #1	
Event #2	
Event #3	
Solution to the problem (resolution)	
Ending (conclusion)	

Organizational Framework for Argumentation (Opinion)

In argumentative writing, the author states an opinion or makes an assertion that might not be universally shared and needs to be defended. The author needs to back up the opinion or assertion with evidence, facts, or beliefs that explain and support the opinion. This supporting text is necessary to persuade the reader to agree with the piece's opinion or assertion.

Words that are often found in argumentative writing include *therefore, because, so, above all, the major reason, most important, it should be noted that,* and *I believe that.*

Planning Frame for Opinion Writing #1

The best book our class has read is _____. I liked it because

_____ . It was

better than _____ because _____ . I

especially liked the part where _____ . I believe that

everybody should read it.

Planning Frame for Opinion Writing #2

My favorite holiday is _____ . I like it because

_____ . On

_____, we do special things like

_____ . It is better than

_____ because

_____ . It is my favorite holiday.

Organizational Framework for Explanatory or Informational Writing

Explanatory writing seeks to explain factual information or observations about a controlling or central idea. By grade 3, students are expected to be able to gather and analyze information about a topic, select and prioritize ideas about the topic, and write several paragraphs about the topic that will inform the reader about main ideas and details. The details may include examples, comparisons, descriptions, or scenarios. A framework for planning expository writing begins with a good question that will, in turn, prompt a strong main idea statement. Here are some examples:

Key Question	Main Idea Statement
Why are wolves important animals to have in Yellowstone National Park?	Wolves are important animals for the balance of nature in Yellowstone National Park.
Will books become ancient history as computers take over our lives?	There will always be a place for printed books in our lives.
Why is there a national campaign against junk food?	Junk food harms our bodies, our environment, and our wallets.

Once a student has decided on the key question and main idea(s) for an explanatory or informational writing assignment, the student can use a framework such as the following to plan a three-paragraph commentary or report.

Planning Frame for Explanatory/Informational Writing

Title or Topic	
Background information (Why is this important? What question am I going to answer?)	
Paragraph #1: Main idea and notes on details	
Paragraph #2: Main idea and notes on details	
Paragraph #3: Restate what is important	

As students progress in writing development beyond the primary grades, they should exhibit greater independence in topic choice, topic elaboration, and organization of their ideas. However, teachers of grades K–3 need to provide structure for writing assignments, as students in these grades are still gaining the basic foundations that support writing fluency. Good instruction includes explicit teaching of both component skills and the composition process.

Exercise 4.1   Practice Listing

Listing is a way to create idea banks or to remind students of what they already know about a topic. Possibilities are endless, and listing in a group environment can be great fun.

Table 4.1 contains some possible topics for lists. Pick one of these topics, and spend two minutes generating your own list of items that fit within the topic.

List Topic: _____

Items:

Table 4.1   Sample Topics for Creating Lists

Ice cream flavors	Things that smell good	Favorite movies
Green vegetables	Things that smell bad	Olympic events
Possible pets	Color words	Weather events
Worst foods	Words describing water	Fantasy heroes
Things that plug in	Words for moods	Real heroes
Words for tastes	Dog breeds	Baseball teams
Words for shapes	Scariest adventures	Scariest animals
Words for size	Bike/skateboard tricks	Words for attitude
Uses for a brick	Words for texture	Uses for a pillow
Uses for a string	Ways to move on two legs	Words for sounds

Exercise 4.2 | Select Writing Assignment Prompts and Cues

Examine the paintings on the following pages. They are:

- Henry O. Tanner, *The Banjo Lesson*

- Winslow Homer, *Snap the Whip*

- Winslow Homer, *The Gulf Stream*

- Winslow Homer, *A Basket of Clams*

- Pieter Bruegel, *The Wedding Feast*

- Albert Bierstadt, *The Rocky Mountains, Lander's Peak*

- Édouard Marquis, *Creole Women of Color Out Taking the Air*

Select one of the paintings, then discuss how you might use it as a prompt for writing in grades 1 to 3. Write a few reasons to support your opinion about the potential value of the painting as the impetus for a student writing assignment.

_____

_____

_____

_____

_____

_____

_____

_____

_____

_____

_____

_____

_____

The Banjo Lesson, Henry O. Tanner
Reprinted by permission of Hampton University's Archival and Museum Collection,
Hampton University, Hampton, Virginia.

Snap the Whip, Winslow Homer, 1872
Image copyright © The Metropolitan Museum of Art/Art Resource, NY; used by permission.

The Gulf Stream, Winslow Homer, 1899

Image copyright © The Metropolitan Museum of Art/Art Resource, NY; used by permission.

A Basket of Clams, Winslow Homer, 1873

Image copyright © The Metropolitan Museum of Art/Art Resource, NY; used by permission.

The Wedding Feast, Pieter Bruegel
Reprinted by permission of Kunsthistorisches Museum, Vienna, Austria.

Rocky Mountains, Landers Peak, Albert Bierstadt, 1863
Image copyright © The Metropolitan Museum of Art/Art Resource, NY; used by permission.

Creole Women of Color Out Taking the Air, Édouard Marquis

Exercise 4.3 | Collaborate to Determine a Purpose for Student Writing

Pick one of the paintings from the previous exercise. With a partner, briefly role-play a student-teacher interaction in which you work together to identify a purpose and goal for the student's writing about the painting. What did you need to do to come to agreement on the goal?

_____

_____

_____

_____

_____

_____

_____

_____

_____

_____

_____

Teaching the Structure of a Paragraph

By second grade, students should be learning to write paragraphs with a logical structure. That structure can be represented with color coding, a device used by Maureen Aumann in *Step Up to Writing*. Follow along with the presenter to see how each sentence's role in the paragraph can be assigned a color:

- Topic sentence (the overarching idea) = blue (like the sky)
- Transition sentence = green (between blue and yellow)
- Detail sentences = yellow (shining light on the topic)
- Elaborated details = red (like meat)
- Conclusion = different shade of blue

Sample Exercise: Color-Code the Structure of a Paragraph

Teacher: *I'm going to show you a way to think about the job of each of the sentences in a paragraph. When we write a paragraph that explains the reasons why we want something or why something is true, that paragraph begins with a topic sentence. We'll code that sentence blue because it is the overarching "sky" sentence under which everything else goes.*

For example:

Public parks are an important part of our town.

Next, we want to add another sentence that restates and explains the topic sentence further. This sentence will be green because it has some blue in it but it adds a little more information.

Without parks, both people and animals would have less space for necessities.

Next we want to add some details or some reasons why the first sentences are true. We want to tell the reader more about this topic and explain why parks are important. We'll code these sentences yellow because they shine light on the topic.

Without parks, many birds would have no homes.

Parks are our play space.

Parks add beauty to the city.

These sentences still need some more meat. We'll add even more detail under each of our yellow sentences, and we'll use red to code the sentences with the new detail because this is the meat on the bones!

Without parks, many birds would have no homes. They need trees to nest in and grass to put in their nests. Parks are our play space. Where else can we find a swing set or a place to skateboard? Parks also add beauty to the city. I'd rather look at grass and trees than at concrete all the time. Public parks are worth every cent that the city spends on them.

Look closely at the blue-green sentence that we added at the end. It has some of the topic sentence in it, but the words are not exactly the same. We have wrapped up this paragraph by restating the main idea in different words. Now, here's the complete paragraph:

> Public parks are an important part of our town. Without parks, both people and animals would have less space for necessities. Without parks, many birds would have no homes. They need trees to nest in and grass to put in their nests. Parks are our play space. Where else can we find a swing set or a place to skateboard? Parks also add beauty to the city. I'd rather look at grass and trees than at concrete all the time. Public parks are worth every cent that the city spends on them.

Now, let's go back and polish. We can add transition words that connect the ideas and change some words to make the sentences sound better together.

> Public parks are an important part of our town. Without parks, both people and animals would have less space for necessities. For example, many birds would have no homes. Birds of many kinds need trees where they can build nests and grass for lining their nests. Parks are also the space where people and dogs can play. Where else can we find a swing set, a place to skateboard, and a place to take our pets? Finally, parks add beauty to the city. I'd rather look at grass and trees than look at concrete all the time; wouldn't you? Public parks are worth every cent that the city spends on them.

Exercise 4.4 Evaluate a Student Writing Sample, Third Grade

What do you think happened to this third-grade student as he was writing his personal narrative about his "perfect weekend"? What could his teacher have done to help him improve the cohesion and focus of this piece?

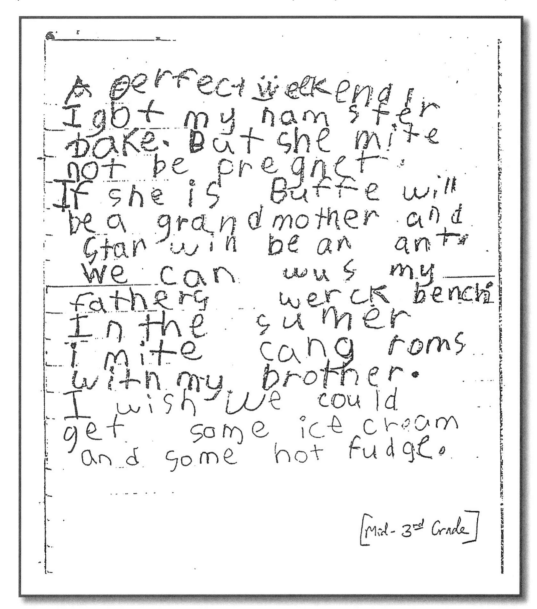

Translation: A Perfect Weekend—I got my hamster back. But she might not be pregnant. If she is, Buffie will be a grandmother and Star will be an aunt. We can use my father's workbench in the summer. I might change rooms with my brother. I wish we could get some ice cream and some hot fudge.

Teaching Students to Prepare to Write

The preparation phase of a writing assignment is as important as the actual transfer of ideas onto paper. Students must have something to say, a goal or purpose, and a vision of the end result. Young students approaching a new writing assignment may be overwhelmed by the choices they must make and the many aspects of writing they must juggle. What part of the topic or experience will they write about? What words will they choose? How will they begin? How many sentences should they write? How are the words spelled? How much information should they include? The prospect of tackling an assignment can be daunting, and it sometimes leaves students chewing their pencils and staring blankly at the empty page. Taking time to prepare and using appropriate planning strategies can be just the antidote for "writer's block" and "drawing a blank."

To keep students from getting stuck before the task even begins, teachers can explain planning strategies and provide a variety of prompts. Think of these as molds that will contain and direct students' thought processes. A list of possibilities is provided in *Table 4.2.*

Table 4.2 Summary of Prompts to Aid Planning

Verbal Preparation Strategies	Nonverbal Prompts
Brainstormed lists	Paintings
Questions to be answered	Illustrations
Word banks	Photographs
Semantic maps of known information	Movies/videos
Story maps	Maps
Partially completed frameworks (cloze sentences)	Objects
Dialogue around shared reading	
Quotes or sayings that evoke response	

All students will put more effort into something they care about. If an assignment is falling flat, rethink its purpose. Writing is hard work. Your goal should be to demonstrate to students that it can be well worth the effort, by helping them gain a sense of accomplishment when they have finished.

Chapter 5 — Enabling Translation

Learner Objectives for Chapter 5

- Distinguish between the two subprocesses of translation.
- Identify techniques to support drafting of a composition.
- Compare writing samples that illustrate different skill levels in first grade.

Warm-Up: Putting Ideas Into Words

Have you ever known a student who seemed to "know a lot" but couldn't come up with the words to express himself or herself? Brainstorm at least five possible causes for this behavior.

1. _____

2. _____

3. _____

4. _____

5. _____

The Two Aspects of Translation

The act of putting words on a page draws on two distinct mental subprocesses. After the writer conjures up ideas and plans the structure that a written piece will take, he or she must select words and phrases to express those ideas. A mental "text generator" is activated as thoughts are translated into words to be written down. Then, once the words and sentences are generated, they must be held in working memory long enough to be transcribed into written text. (See *Figure 5.1*, next page.)

Transcription calls on many subskills, including sequential and coordinated finger movements and motor memories, for letter formation; phoneme-grapheme associations, for spelling; orthographic memory, for letter sequences in words; and memory, for punctuation symbols. Transcription processes rely on sensory-motor feedback systems, but they are regulated by the attention and executive systems, the "central executive" in the working memory model. The functional processing systems are connected to the language centers of the brain. If practice in spelling and handwriting has automatized transcription—that is, has enabled the student to physically write words without undue effort and attention—then the posterior (back) and lower-level brain systems execute and monitor the production of text. However, if transcription processes are not automatic, the writer uses up valuable attention capacity in working memory just to get the letters and words on the page, which means that the student has less attention available for determining which words to use or for keeping track of the goals of the piece.

Figure 5.1 Two-Part Translation Process

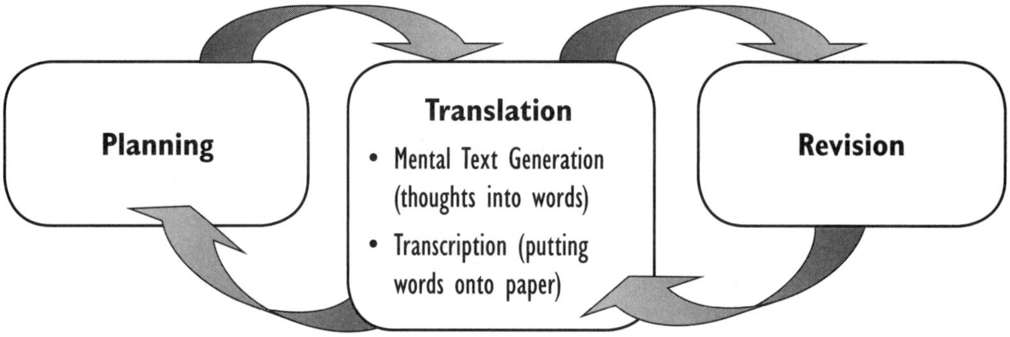

Transfer of Thoughts Into Words

Translating ideas into words (mental text generation) depends on the writer's ability to retrieve and select words that are stored in the mental dictionary (the meaning processor). It also depends on the writer's ability to formulate sentences. To choose words that express ideas precisely and with detail, a student needs to "own" a sufficiently large working vocabulary. Vocabulary and background knowledge overlap; those with larger vocabularies know more, and those who know more have wider and deeper vocabularies (Hirsch, 2006). Students with limited vocabularies and background knowledge write fewer words overall, use fewer precise or unusual words when they do write, and overuse common words that carry little meaning. To express ideas completely and precisely, a writer needs a well-stocked mental dictionary[1].

How can we ensure that students have the necessary words for expressing their thoughts? First, the curriculum itself must have a strong vocabulary-development component and must include incentives for students to read widely in varied texts. In addition, after students are thoroughly prepared to write about a specific topic, teachers can support their word choice skills by:

- Charting and categorizing key terms to prompt the use of richer vocabulary related to the topic (*Table 5.1* provides an example);
- Putting key words on a writer's bookmark for handy reference; and

---

1   Module 4 of LETRS is focused solely on vocabulary development and instruction.

- Generating wall charts or reference cards showing words that students can substitute for common, overused words.

Table 5.1 Vocabulary Words for Reports About Rain Forest Frogs

Look Like	Touch/Feel	Actions	Body Parts	Behavior
flashy	moist	climb	webbed feet	lay eggs
fantastic	sticky	cling	long tongues	eat insects
striped	smooth	glide	poisonous skin	stalk prey
dotted	clear	croak		don't swim
colorful				
camouflaged				

Transcription

Early writing instruction should aim to develop habits and skills of transcription. Students can gain command of handwriting, spelling, and sentence production even as they learn to generate ideas, organize them, and put them down on paper. Young students may need considerable assistance to be able to generate the words they want. A number of strategies can keep them from "blocking" as they start to write. In addition to the approaches discussed in Chapter 4, these strategies include:

- Talking out ideas before writing them down;
- Keeping the original plan and goals in view;
- Talking through ideas midstream if students get "stuck"; and
- Supplying transcription supports such as a list of correct spellings for commonly used words.

Writing a Draft

Students' first draft of a writing project should be treated as just that—a first go. Writing is difficult, and students will inevitably make mistakes. Establish the expectation that students can always improve their drafts and that good writers revisit their work many times to revise, edit, and polish. Additional tips for getting early writers started on a first draft:

- Have students use lined, yellow paper.
- Have them use a pencil with an eraser—not a pen.
- Encourage them to leave a blank line after each line of text so that editing will be easier.
- Keep word lists and organizational aids in view.
- Allow students as much time as they need.
- For students in late first grade or in second grade, provide a template for a simple paragraph. Model paragraph construction many times, demonstrating how to write a topic sentence, provide supporting details, and develop a closing sentence.

Exercise 5.1   Evaluate First-Grade Writing Samples

Look at the following writing samples of first-grade students who have been assessed using the *Dynamic Indicators of Basic Early Literacy Skills* (DIBELS). In what ways do the words, sentences, and overall quality of language and ideas correspond to the students' status as "low-risk," "some-risk," and "at-risk" learners?

Student #1, C.P. Composition in grade 1, early January.

Rated low-risk on DIBELS measures. C.P. is doing extremely well in letter naming (99th percentile), phoneme segmentation (99th percentile), nonsense word reading (98th percentile), and word-use fluency (76th percentile).

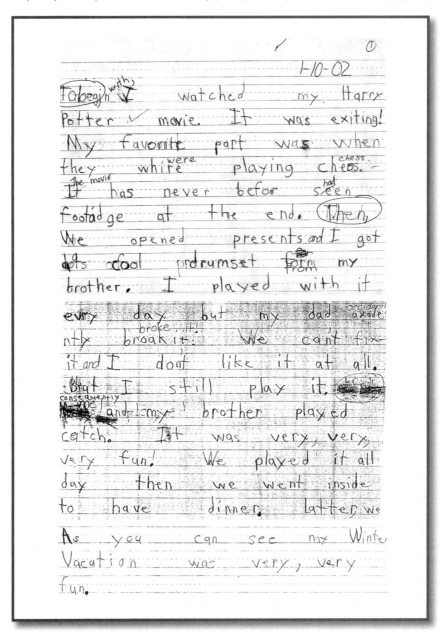

Exercise 5.1 (continued)

Student #2, N.C. Composition in grade 1, early December.

At some risk, according to DIBELS measures. Rated in the 64th percentile on letter naming, 15th percentile on phoneme segmentation, 21st percentile on nonsense word reading, and 44th percentile on word-use fluency. N.C. receives a half-hour per day of extra small-group help with multisensory structured language, in addition to a classroom Open Court program. N.C. also works on CD-ROM with Lindamood LIPS Program and Earobics training in phonology.

```
12-7-03
My thankgiving was fun.
Frst thankgiving was a
blast. We had it at
my gramas huse.
We had cake for
luch and it was
good. then after
it was fun at
my cusins huse.
but afder We had to
go home. but
Ulee I come
hose With my toys.
```

```
my favrt food was cake
We had so much
fun do you no
W
```

(continued)

Exercise 5.1   (continued)

Student #3, J.D.: Composition in grade 1, January.

J.D. is considered an at-risk student, needing intensive support. J.D. has been on an IEP since kindergarten, receiving one-on-one tutoring and small-group instruction. Rated in the 21st percentile on letter naming, the 4th percentile on phoneme awareness, the 31st percentile on nonsense word reading, and the 26th percentile on word use fluency.

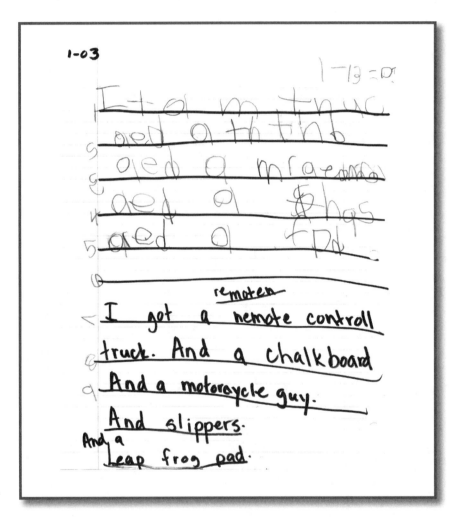

How do these examples demonstrate the relationship between composition quality, composition fluency, and automatization of skill at the level of letter knowledge, letter formation, phoneme awareness, phonics, and vocabulary?

Overcoming Barriers to Effective Translation

Struggling writers are commonly frustrated by the demands of the translation process. These include two important subprocesses: translating their ideas into words and then transcribing those words onto the page. The first subprocess, corralling the words necessary to express intended meanings, requires an adequate vocabulary and the ability to fluently retrieve words from memory. The second subprocess, transcription, depends on sufficient mastery of handwriting, spelling, capitalization, usage, and punctuation—the orthographic skills that distinguish writing from speaking.

There are several ways in which teachers can support students struggling with the translation phase of writing. Most important, they should ensure that students have already elaborated on their ideas before they begin translation, and they should make sure students have ready access to vocabulary words on the topic they are writing about.

Teachers who provide supports for the translation process will see better results. Offer vocabulary words in the form of lists, semantic maps, word banks, personal bookmarks, thesauruses, continuing dialogue, and even dictation if a student is stuck. Remember that a young writer's working memory is often overloaded, so providing lots of support during the actual writing of a composition is entirely fair.

Chapter 6 Review, Revision, and Publication

Learner Objectives for Chapter 6
- Define *review* and *revision*.
- Examine techniques for supporting review, revision, and publishing.
- Consider the pros and cons of technology-assisted writing instruction.
- Plan a writing lesson.

Warm-Up: How Do You Get Students to Revise?
What procedures are you currently using that help students evaluate and revise their written work?

_____

_____

_____

_____

_____

_____

Review and Revision

The three phases of composition—planning, translation, and reviewing—are recursive; the writer moves back and forth among them, in no particular order, once writing has begun. *Review* and *revision*, the two components of the reviewing phase of composition, occur both during and after the generation of text. Review is the process of looking as objectively as possible at one's own work from the perspective of the reader, keeping in mind that the reader needs conventional transcription of language and clarity of expression in order to understand. Revision involves changing a draft's word choice, sentence structure, or overall organization; expanding on, adding, or deleting ideas; and altering the print symbols themselves.

These processes, through which writers polish a draft before publication, represent a never-ending task, even for accomplished authors. Review and revision never stop until the work is published, and even then, the writer often rues the final product!

Why Young Writers Resist Revision

Young students who are just learning to write are often resistant to revising a written product. They want the assignment to be over and finished so that they can move on. Young writers who put great effort into generating the first draft of an assignment because their transcription skills are not yet well-developed or automatized want the work to be acceptable as is. They feel frustrated at the thought of having to rewrite, especially if rewriting focuses on correcting errors of transcription. Students learn revision in small steps, with frequent modeling on the part of the instructor, so the teacher's expectations must be imposed gradually.

Overcoming Resistance in a Beginning Writer

One path around students' natural resistance is to focus first on content, not on transcription errors. When helping a student review and revise a particular piece, begin by responding to the communicative intent of the writer. Did the writer try to share an experience or idea of importance to him or her? Did the writer introduce the topic clearly? What does the piece tell you about that experience or idea? Did the writer tell you enough about it? Did the writer supply adequate detail? Did the writer choose strong words? Are the ideas clearly expressed?

Next, focus on organization. Did the writer stick to his or her plan and do a good job of sequencing the sentences? Do the sentences hang together? Does the piece include transition words? Does it have a discernible paragraph structure?

Only after addressing issues of content and organization should you focus on transcription accuracy. Help the student identify any misspelled words that he or she should already know how to spell by virtue of previous instruction. Supply the correct spelling of any words that the student has not yet encountered in spelling lessons. Even if spelling corrections come at the end of a review and revision discussion, they are still important. Except in the very early stages of writing, expect correct spelling. Don't let students slip a lot of "invented" spelling into a final draft without providing corrections.

Supporting Students' Review and Revision

As the brain matures and skills develop, students attain the cognitive perspective necessary to evaluate their own writing from the point of view of someone in their prospective audience. To cultivate students' awareness of their audience, have them share their writing with others who can react to it. Over time, a writer's working memory systems become able to simultaneously monitor the words that are being written and the words that have been written. Writers become capable of thinking about the goal they began with, even as they are writing. And as they have more words to draw on, more fluency with sentences, and more knowledge of writing conventions, students can begin to compare drafts with an inwardly held standard. However, this kind of perspective-taking is unusual before the intermediate grades.

Elementary students require support and direction as they proofread for grammar, punctuation, capitalization, and spelling. Obviously, in order to proofread, a student must have solid skills in each of these areas. For many students, the incidental practice that comes from proofreading their own work is not sufficient to learn all the important conventions of language and symbolization in writing. Some procedures that support and assist students in evaluating their writing include:

Sentence Check

Read an incomplete or awkward sentence aloud, and ask students whether it sounds right. Then create a complete sentence from the fragment, using a sentence-builder chart or a visual coding system to identify what part of the sentence is missing. For example, read: "But she might not be pregnant." Ask: "Does that sound like a whole sentence that can stand alone? What's missing? When you start a sentence with *but*, you must attach it to a main clause. What could the main clause be in this case?"

Sentence Lifting

Select two or three sentences from students' work; write them on a chart or chalkboard; and proofread them together with the class. Use these sentences to remind the class about skills they have already learned. Focus on word choice, especially the subject noun and the main verb. Look for opportunities to combine simple sentences into a compound or complex sentence.

Personal Proofreading Checklists

Have students keep personal proofreading checklists on bookmarks or in folders. Limit the number of corrections students are expected to make on their own usage of spelling, grammar, punctuation, and capitalization. Focus on reminders of what the students have already been taught.

Author's Chair (second grade and up)

Each day, ask a few students to read their work aloud to the whole class or a small group. Situate an "author's chair" that students can occupy while they share their writing. Guide the class or small group into making constructive comments about substance, style, and word choice in the shared writing.

Peer Conferences

Peer conferencing is enjoyable for students, but they must be taught how to offer constructive feedback after listening to a peer read his or her writing. Supervise these sessions; set ground rules for students to comment on one another's work. Discourage global statements such as "I liked it." Rather, encourage comments about the writer's choice of specific words, how interesting the listeners found specific parts of the writing, whether they need more information, whether the draft needs a conclusion, and so forth. See *Figure 6.1* for examples of effective comments from student reviewers.

Note that during a conference, the writer holds onto the work, keeps control of it, and decides which of the suggested changes to make.

Figure 6.1   Dialoguing With an Author

I liked the part where you said _____ .

I thought the best words you used were _____ .

Which part do you like? _____ .

I wish you said a lot more about _____ .

Did you think about something that you want to add?

_____

_____

Exercise 6.1   Give Corrective Feedback

Suppose that you decided to lift the following two sentences from a third-grader's writing.

we can wus my fathers werck bench

in the sumer I mite cang roms with my brother

You put these sentences on an overhead projector in order to coach students through a proofreading and editing session. What prompts or questions will you use to help the students edit and revise these sentences?

Questions:

_____

_____

_____

_____

Assistive Technology

In his review of technological tools that support planning, writing, and revision, MacArthur (2009) concludes that electronic aids offer a mix of advantages and disadvantages. However, most research on the use of computer-assisted instruction has been conducted with intermediate, middle school, and high school students. Little guidance is available regarding the pros and cons of using computers in teaching young students to write.

Students who have learning disabilities and writing problems struggle with all aspects of the task. Planning, translating, and reviewing are all difficult for them. Students with learning disabilities are less strategic through all phases of writing, and they tend to focus on superficialities when they revise. Because their needs seem overwhelming, educators may be tempted to turn to technology for solutions. Spell checkers, grammar checkers, word processors, and even speech recognition and word prediction software can aid students in the transcription phase of writing. (Word prediction software guesses which word the student is trying to type, based on a few letters and the sentence context.) Moreover, outlining and concept mapping programs are available to help with planning. Each of these, while helpful, demands a skill set in its own right.

MacArthur (2009) points out that word processing has been proven helpful in bolstering the quality and quantity of writing among low-achieving students in grades 4 to 12, but that the effect is much smaller among students whose performance is at grade level. In order to benefit from word processing in writing assignments, a student must be able to type at least 20 words per minute. Otherwise, handwriting is the better medium. In addition, teachers cannot assume that access to a word processing program means students will effectively revise their work. Revision must be modeled, prompted, and supervised, and students need guidance in learning to focus on substantive issues of expressive quality.

Successful use of a spell checker requires about a fifth-grade level of spelling ability (Joshi, Treiman, Carreker, & Moats, 2008-2009). Spell checkers can improve a student's overall outcomes, but they are not a total solution. Really poor spellers often cannot detect homophone errors or choose the correct word from among the options that a spell checker offers.

Speech-recognition software may be helpful for adults who cannot write because of a physical disability, but the technology has serious limitations for students in an elementary classroom. First, the programs recognize accurately only some of the words that a person is saying. Second, the computer must be told when to punctuate and capitalize. Third, the user must be in a quiet place, and must receive several hours' training in the use of the software. Studies show greater success at the middle school and high school levels, and in situations where an individual user is working alone.

Word prediction programs have been shown to help 9- to 11-year-old students with severe spelling disabilities. Other students, such as those with attention deficits, might also benefit from this technology, but little research has been done with these populations.

In general, the best approach is to teach handwritten production of written language in the early grades. By the intermediate grades, for students who meet a typing fluency and accuracy standard, word processing and related tools may offer an advantage for writing quality.

Publishing Students' Work

Publishing is the end point of the whole writing process. Publishing a student's written work means presenting it to an audience. Common methods for publishing elementary students' work include:

- Posting corrected and neatly presented work in a public place;
- Producing books that are anthologies of student stories or reports, and laminating the pages so that they last; or
- Keeping each student's writing in a personal writing folder so that you, the student, and parents can see progress over the course of the year.

Not all work needs to be published; some may remain in a student's writing folder, unfinished or unpolished. However, publishing can be a good motivator for engaging young writers in an assignment and then encouraging them to review and revise their work.

Exercise 6.2	Review Possible Writing Lessons Prompted by a Reading

In preparation for planning your own upcoming writing lessons, examine the following three writing assignments, any of which would be appropriate after students read the story "A Home for Lizzie," which we studied in Modules 4 and 6. Work through these models with your presenter.

1. **Lists and Categories: Backyard Discoveries**

   List some surprises you have found in your backyard or in the neighborhood around your house.

   Now, let's put your discoveries into categories. If you find something new today or tomorrow, we'll decide what category it goes in—and add it to our list!

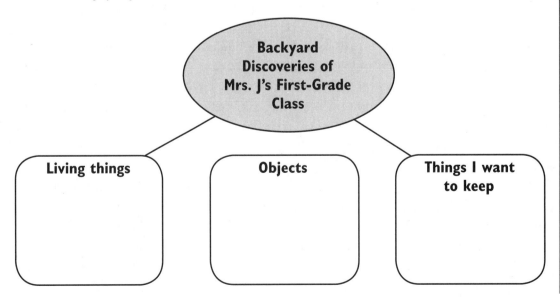

Exercise 6.2   (continued)

2. **Description: My Favorite Place to Be**

[Model of a brainstorming session to prompt description] *Today, class, we will all be thinking about our favorite place to be and finding good words that describe how that place feels, looks, sounds, and smells, and why we like to be there.*

My favorite place to be is on my couch, in front of my fireplace, at home with a good book in the evening. It's quiet and peaceful. I feel safe, relaxed, and content there. What's your favorite place?

Call on some volunteers. Remind them to tell you words that describe the feelings, sights, sounds, smells, and actions in their favorite place.

I feel	I see	I hear	I taste	I do	I smell

Now, write some sentences about your favorite place. You can use these sentence starters if you like, or you can make your own sentences:

My favorite place to be is _____.

When I am there, I like to _____.

I go there (when) _____.

I feel _____.

I hear _____.

I see _____. It's my favorite place!

(continued)

Exercise 6.2 (continued)

When you are ready, find a partner and share what you have written. Let your partner ask you three questions about your favorite place. Then see if there is anything else you would like to add to your description.

3. **Composing a Personal Narrative**

   The little girl in our story ("A Home for Lizzie") found a creature in her backyard. At first she wanted to keep it. Then she realized that the creature was happier and more likely to live if she let it go.

   Have you ever found something that you decided to let go or give back? Do you remember what made you decide to let it go or give it back? Do you remember how you felt about that? Tell what you did and what happened. First, talk about your idea with a partner. Then, plan the parts of your personal narrative.

Title or Topic
Beginning (where, when, who) "One day ..."
Events that happened (First, then, next, finally)
How the story ends. How it felt to you or the last thing that happened.

Exercise 6.3 | Plan a Writing Lesson

Select one of the paintings that we reviewed in Chapter 4. Working individually or in a small group, plan a writing lesson for one day that follows the format introduced in Chapter 1 and repeated below. Identify or describe the student(s) you have in mind as you plan this lesson.

5–10 Minute Warm-Up to Build Transcription Fluency

Includes student activities such as:

- Forming a few letters, using numbered arrow cues, tracing, verbalizing, or writing from memory, then evaluating accuracy.

- Producing the alphabet, in sequence, one or two times per session, until fluency is achieved.

- Writing graphemes for dictated phonemes (vowels and consonants), including letter combinations such as vowel teams and digraphs.

- Combining onsets and rimes to write whole syllables.

- Writing high-frequency words to dictation—a few at a time, singly, or in sentences—saying the letters while writing each word.

10–20 Minutes: Compose With Teacher Modeling and Assistance

Planning

- Establish the goal of the activity.

- Help students establish the topic; use prompts as appropriate.

- Build or elicit topic knowledge from students.

- Show or create a model of a finished product.

- Generate and list ideas for writing.

- Help students arrange ideas in order.

- Think, pair, share: Have students share with a friend before writing.

Drafting (translating ideas into words and translating words into writing)

- Compose in dialogue with the students, writing down what they say on a chart, overhead, or cue cards.

- Begin sentences with the students, and have them complete the sentences.

- Encourage students to prompt themselves with self-talk or partner-talk.

Reviewing and revising (as appropriate after conferences)

- Have students share writing with peers or adults.

- Talk over what can be added, deleted, elaborated, or rearranged.

- Lift one or two sentences from a student's work to demonstrate proofreading and editing.

(continued)

Exercise 6.3 (continued)

Sample Lesson Plan

For which student(s): _____

_____

5–10 Minute Warm-Up to Build Transcription Fluency

Which activity? _____

_____

Using what prompts or materials? _____

_____

With what intended outcome? _____

_____

10–20 Minutes: Compose With Teacher Modeling and Assistance

First, select the phase of the writing process that the lesson will emphasize. Decide whether you are teaching the planning, translating, or reviewing phase. Then, focus your objectives appropriately.

Focus or purpose: _____

_____

Activity: _____

_____

Prompts, materials: _____

_____

Intended outcomes (objectives): _____

_____

A Comprehensive Approach to Beginning Writing Instruction

Building a "writing brain," according to Berninger and Richards (2002), means building a proficient language system that embodies all necessary functional components. All the mental and linguistic processors that support listening, speaking, and reading are employed in writing, with the addition of other sensory, motor, attention, memory, and executive functions.

The mental juggling act of writing is daunting: We must hold in mind what we want to say, recall specific symbolic forms, keep the goal and organization in mind, and monitor whether the writing is communicating effectively to the reader. This combination of activities heavily taxes working memory, which is a limited-capacity processor. In other words, only so much memory is available to devote to any one task. To become a proficient writer, a student must automatize skills to free up memory space for other, higher-level writing processes, in much the same way that we must sometimes free up space on a computer desktop. The conscious mind needs "desktop space" for all the higher-level problem-solving and decision-making that composition demands.

As the executive system juggles its various jobs, it becomes vulnerable to disruption, overload, and faulty processing, especially in the non-expert writer. Young students may seem to have learned component skills, such as spelling or creating paragraphs, but when we demand too many skills at once during composition, the whole system can fail—just as too many appliances plugged into one outlet can cause system overload.

Building a cognitive system that effectively supports writing requires a teacher to strengthen component skills so that students can use them while paying less attention to each one, increasing the juggling capacity in their mental desktop and expanding their repertoire of problem-solving strategies (Graham, MacArthur, & Fitzgerald, 2007; Scardamalia & Bereiter, 1986).

The primary grades afford an opportunity to teach the most critical skills early and well. This is also the ideal time to use structured, supported methods to acquaint students with higher-level writing skills that they will master much later on a developmental continuum. Extensive research has shown that if the foundations of handwriting, spelling, and sentence fluency are established early, composition quality and length improves throughout grades 2, 3, and 4 (Berninger & Wolf, 2009; McCutchen, 1996; Moats, Foorman, & Taylor, 2006). Failure to establish transcription skills in an elementary-level writer whose language skills are otherwise normal compromises the student's overall writing development. Transcription capabilities facilitate composition quality and length.

To teach young students to write, take these actions:
- Show them what you want (model).
- Teach handwriting and spelling to the point of automatic and accurate usefulness.
- Teach component skills, including sentence structure, before requiring their application.
- Give students prompts for ideas and words.
- Show them how to organize their thoughts before writing.
- Give the draft as much structure as it needs.
- Provide the opportunity for audience response, emphasizing the message in the writing first.
- Provide proofreading and editing assistance.
- Publish in the real world.

References

Abbott, R.D., Berninger, V.W., & Fayol, M. (2010). Longitudinal relationships of levels of language in writing and between writing and reading in grades 1 to 7. *Journal of Educational Psychology, 102*(2), 281–298.

Allen, K.A., Neuhaus, G.F., & Beckwith, M.C. (2005). Alphabet knowledge: Letter recognition, naming, and sequencing. In J. Birsh (Ed.), *Multisensory Teaching of Basic Language Skills, 2nd Edition* (pp. 113–150). Baltimore, MD: Paul H. Brookes Publishing.

Baddeley, A.D. (2001). Is working memory still working? *American Psychologist, 56,* 848-864.

Bain, A.M., Bailet, L.L., & Moats, L.C. (2001). *Written language disorders: Theory into practice.* Austin, TX: PRO-ED.

Beck, R., Conrad, D., & Anderson, P. (2009). *Practicing basic skills in reading: One-minute fluency builders series.* Longmont, CO: Sopris West Educational Services.

Berninger, V.W. (1999). Coordinating transcription and text generation in working memory during composing: Automatized and constructive processes. *Learning Disability Quarterly, 22,* 99–112.

Berninger, V.W., & Richards, T.L. (2002). *Brain literacy for educators and psychologists.* Amsterdam: Academic Press.

Berninger, V.W., & Wolf, B.J. (2009). *Teaching students with dyslexia and dysgraphia: Lessons from teaching and science.* Baltimore, MD: Paul H. Brookes Publishing.

Ehri, L.C., & Snowling, M.J. (2004). Developmental variation in word recognition. In C.A. Stone, E.R. Silliman, B.J. Ehren, & K. Apel (Eds.), *Handbook of language and literacy: Development and disorders* (pp. 433–460). New York, NY: Guilford Publications.

Foorman, B.R., Petscher, Y., Lefsky, E.B., & Toste, J.R. (2010). Reading first in Florida: Five years of improvement. *Journal of Literacy Research, 42,* 71–93.

Graham, S. (1997). Executive control in the revising of students with learning and writing difficulties. *Journal of Educational Psychology, 89,* 223–234.

Graham, S. (1999). Handwriting and spelling instruction for students with learning disabilities: A review. *Learning Disability Quarterly, 22*(2), 78–98.

Graham, S., Berninger, V.W., Abbott, R.D., Abbott, S.P., & Whitaker, D. (1997). The role of mechanics in composing of elementary school students: A new methodological approach. *Journal of Educational Psychology, 89*(1), 170–182.

Graham, S., MacArthur, C.A., & Fitzgerald, J. (Eds.). (2007). *Best practices in writing instruction: Solving problems in the teaching of literacy.* New York, NY: Guilford Publications.

Graham, S., & Perin, D. (2007). *Writing next: Effective strategies to improve writing of adolescents in middle and high schools: A report to Carnegie Corporation of New York.* Washington, DC: Alliance for Excellent Education.

Graham, S., & Weintraub, N. (1996). A review of handwriting research: Progress and prospects from 1980 to 1994. *Educational Psychology Review, 8*(1), 7–87.

Hayes, J.R., & Flower, L.S. (1980). Identifying the organization of the writing processes. In L.W. Gregg & E.R. Steinberg (Eds.), *Cognitive processes in writing* (pp. 3–30). Hillsdale, NJ: Erlbaum.

Hirsch, E.D. (2006). *The knowledge deficit: Closing the shocking education gap for American children.* Boston, MA: Houghton Mifflin.

Hochman, J.C. (2009). *Teaching basic writing skills: Strategies for effective expository writing instruction.* Longmont, CO: Sopris West Educational Services.

Hooper, B., & Moats, L.C. (2010). *Primary spelling by pattern, Level 2.* Longmont, CO: Sopris West Educational Services.

Jacobs, V.A. (1997). The use of connectives in low-income children's writing: Linking reading, writing, and language skill development. In L.R. Putnam (Ed.), *Readings on language and literacy: Essays in honor of Jeanne S. Chall* (pp. 100–130). Cambridge, MA: Brookline Books.

Jenkins, J.R., Johnson, E., & Hileman, J. (2004). When is reading also writing: Sources of individual differences on the new reading performance assessments. *Scientific Studies of Reading Journal, 8*(2), 125–151.

Joshi, R.M., Treiman, R., Carreker, S., & Moats, L.C. (2008-2009). How words cast their spell: Spelling is an integral part of learning the language, not a matter of memorization. *American Educator, 32*(4), 6–16, 42–43.

MacArthur, C.A. (2009). Using technology to teach composing to struggling writers. In G.A. Troia (Ed.), *Instruction and assessment for struggling writers: Evidence-based practices* (pp. 243–268). New York, NY: Guilford Publications.

McCutchen, D. (1996). A capacity theory of writing: Working memory in composition. *Educational Psychology Review, 8*(3), 299–325.

Moats, L.C. (2010). *Speech to Print: Language essentials for teachers, 2nd Edition.* Baltimore, MD: Paul H. Brookes Publishing.

Moats, L.C. (1995). *Spelling: Development, disability, and instruction.* Baltimore, MD: York Press.

Moats, L.C., Foorman, B.R., & Taylor, W.P. (2006). How quality of writing instruction impacts high-risk fourth graders' writing. *Reading and Writing: An Interdisciplinary Journal, 19,* 363–391.

National Assessment of Educational Progress. (2008). *The Nation's Report Card: Writing 2007, NCES 2008-468.* Washington, DC: U.S. Department of Education, Institute of Education Sciences, National Center for Education Statistics. Retrieved April 11, 2011, from http://nces.ed.gov/nationsreportcard/pdf/main2007/2008468.pdf

National Assessment of Educational Progress. (2010). *The Nation's Report Card: Reading 2009, NCES 2010-458.* Washington, DC: U.S. Department of Education, Institute of Education Sciences, National Center for Education Statistics. Retrieved April 11, 2011, from http://nces.ed.gov/nationsreportcard/pdf/main2009/2010458.pdf

National Commission on Writing for America's Families, Schools, and Colleges, The. (2004). *Writing: A ticket to work ... or a ticket out: A survey of business leaders.* New York, NY: College Entrance Examination Board. Retrieved April 1, 2011, from www.writingcommission. org/prod_downloads/writingcom/writing-ticket-to-work.pdf

National Commission on Writing for America's Families, Schools, and Colleges, The. (2005). *Writing: A powerful message from state government.* New York, NY: College Entrance Examination Board. Retrieved April 1, 2011, from www.writingcommission.org/prod_downloads/writingcom/powerful-message-from-state.pdf

National Institute of Child Health and Human Development. (2000). *Report of the National Reading Panel: Teaching children to read: An evidence-based assessment of the scientific research literature on reading and its implications for reading instruction.* Washington, DC: U.S. Government Printing Office.

Paulson, L.H., & Moats, L.C. (2009). *LETRS for early childhood educators.* Longmont, CO: Cambium Learning® Sopris West®.

Persky, H.R., Daane, M.C., & Jin, Y. (2003). *The nation's report card: Writing 2002, NCES 2003-529.* Washington, DC: U.S. Department of Education, Institute of Education Sciences, National Center for Education Statistics. Retrievable from http://nces.ed.gov/nationsreportcard/pdf/main2002/2003529.pdf

Scardamalia, M., & Bereiter, C. (1986). Research on written composition. In M.C. Wittrock (Ed.), *Handbook of research on teaching: A project of the American Educational Research Association, 3rd Edition* (pp. 778–803). New York, NY: MacMillan.

Scott, C.M. (2004). Syntactic contributions to literacy development. In C.A. Stone, E.R. Silliman, B.J. Ehren, & K. Apel (Eds.), *Handbook of language and literacy: Development and disorders* (pp. 340–362). New York, NY: Guilford Publications.

Troia, G.A. (Ed.). (2009). *Instruction and assessment for struggling writers: Evidence-based practices.* New York, NY: Guilford Publications.

Troia, G.A., Lin, S.C., Monroe, B.W., & Cohen, S. (2009). The effects of writing workshop instruction on the performance and motivation of good and poor writers. In G.A. Troia (Ed.), *Instruction and assessment for struggling writers: Evidence-based practices* (pp. 77–112). New York, NY: Guilford Publications.

Vanderberg, R., & Swanson, H.L. (2007). Which components of working memory are important in the writing process? *Reading and Writing, 20,* 721–752.

Weiser, B. (2010). *Examining the synergistic relationship of encoding and decoding instruction and its effect on first graders struggling with reading.* A dissertation presented to the graduate faculty of Southern Methodist University (Unpublished manuscript).

Wolf, B.J. (2005). Teaching handwriting. In J.R. Birsh (Ed.), *Multisensory teaching of basic language skills, 2nd Edition* (pp. 413–438). Baltimore, MD: Paul H. Brookes Publishing.

Instructional Resources for Multisensory Instruction of Grammar and Beginning Writing

Multisensory Grammar and Written Composition—Suzanne Carreker, Neuhaus Center, Houston, TX (www.neuhaus.org)

Project Read: Framing Your Thoughts Sentence Structure Guide and Companion DVDs Victoria Greene and Mary Lee Enfield, Language Circle Enterprises, Bloomington, Minnesota (www.projectread.com)

Step Up to Writing: Hands-On Strategies for Writing, Thinking, and Content Learning—Maureen Auman, Cambium Learning® Sopris, Longmont, Colorado (www.soprislearning.com)

Spelling by Pattern, Levels 1–3—Ellen Javernick, Betty Hooper, Louisa Moats, Cambium Learning® Sopris, Longmont, Colorado (www.soprislearning.com)

Teaching Basic Writing Skills: Strategies for Effective Expository Writing Instruction—Judith Hochman, Cambium Learning® Sopris, Longmont, Colorado (www.soprislearning.com)

Word Shapes (formerly called Sentence Builders)—ARK Institute, Tacoma, Washington (www.arkinst.org)

Appendices

Appendix A
Common Core State Standards for Writing

Kindergartners	Grade 1 Students
Text Types and Purposes	
1. Use a combination of drawing, dictating, and writing to compose opinions in which they tell a reader the name of a book or the topic they are "writing" about and give an opinion about the topic.	1. Write opinions in which they introduce the topic or the name of the book they are writing about, state an opinion, and provide a reason for their opinion.
2. Use a combination of drawing, dictating, and writing to compose **informative** and **explanatory** texts in which they name what they are "writing" about and share some information about it.	2. Write **informative** and **explanatory** texts in which they name a topic, supply some facts relevant to the topic, and provide some sense of closure.
3. Use a combination of drawing, dictating, and writing to **narrate** a single event or several loosely linked events, tell about the events in order that they occurred, and provide a reaction to what happened.	3. Write **narratives** in which they include at least two or more appropriately sequenced events, use time cue words to signal event order, and provide some details and a sense of closure.
Production and Distribution of Writing	
4. (Begins in grade 3.)	4. (Begins in grade 3.)
5. With guidance and support from adults, add details to strengthen writing as needed through revision.	5. With guidance and support from adults, add details to strengthen writing as needed through revision.
6. (Begins in grade 2.)	6. (Begins in grade 2.)

(continued)

Research to Build Knowledge	
7. (Begins in grade 1.)	7. Participate in shared research and writing projects (e.g., exploring a number of books on a given topic).
8. Gather information from experiences or provided text resources to answer a specific question.	8. Gather information from experiences or provided text resources to answer a specific question.

Text Types and Purposes	
Grade 2 Students	**Grade 3 Students**
1. Write **opinions** in which they introduce the topic or book(s) directly, state an opinion, provide reasons and details to support opinions, use words to link opinions and reason(s) (e.g., *because, and, also*), and provide a sense of closure.	1. Write **opinions** in which they: a. Introduce the topic or book(s) directly, state an opinion relative to the topic, and create an organizing structure that lists reasons. b. Provide reasons that support the opinions. c. Use appropriate words to link opinions and reason(s) (e.g., *because, therefore, in order to, since, for example*). d. Provide a sense of closure.
2. Write **informative** and **explanatory** texts in which they introduce a topic, use facts and definitions to develop points, present similar information together using headers to signal groupings when appropriate, and provide a concluding sentence or section.	2. Write **informative** and **explanatory** pieces in which they: a. Introduce a topic and create an organizational structure that presents similar information together. b. Provide some details to develop points. c. Use linking words (e.g., *also, another, and, more*) to connect ideas within categories of information. d. Include a concluding sentence or section.

3. Write **narratives** in which they recount a well-elaborated event or series of events; use temporal words and phrases to signal event order; include details to tell what the narrator did, thought, and felt; and provide closure.	3. Write **narratives** in which they: a. Establish a situation, introduce a narrator and/or characters, and organize an event sequence that unfolds naturally. b. Employ dialogue and descriptions of characters' actions, thoughts, and feelings. c. Use temporal words and phrases to signal event sequence. d. Provide a sense of closure.

Production and Distribution of Writing	
4. (Begins in grade 3.)	4. (See page 21 of Common Core State Standards for Writing.)
5. With guidance and support from adults, strengthen writing as needed by revising and editing.	5. With guidance and support from adults, strengthen writing as needed by revising and editing.
6. With guidance from adults, use technology to produce writing.	6. With guidance and support from adults, use technology to produce and publish writing.

Research to Build Knowledge	
7. Participate in shared research and writing projects (e.g., exploring a number of books on a given topic).	7. Perform short, focused research tasks that build knowledge about a topic.
8. Gather information from experiences or provided text resources to answer a specific question.	8. Gather information from experiences as well as print and digital resources, take simple notes on sources, and sort evidence into provided categories.

Appendix B
Common Core State Standards for Language

Kindergartners	Grade 1 Students
Conventions in Writing and Speaking	

1. Observe conventions of grammar and usage.
 	
   a. Print most upper and lowercase letters.
 	
   b. Write a letter or letters for most consonant and short-vowel sounds (phonemes).
 	
   c. Form regular plural nouns orally by adding /s/ or /es/ (e.g., **dog, dogs; wish, wishes**) when speaking.
 	
   d. Understand and use the most frequently occurring prepositions in English (e.g., *to, from, in, out, on, off, for, of, by, with*) when speaking.
 	
   e. Produce and expand complete sentences in shared language and writing activities.
 	
   f. Understand and use question words (e.g., *who, what, where, when, why, how*) in discussions.
	1. Observe conventions of grammar and usage.
	
	   a. Print all upper and lowercase letters.
	
	   b. Use singular and plural nouns with matching verbs in simple sentences (e.g., **He hops. We hop.**).
	
	   c. Use subject, object, and possessive pronouns in speaking and writing (e.g., *I, me, my; they, them, their*).
	
	   d. Use verbs to convey a sense of past, present, and future in writing and speaking (e.g., **Yesterday I walked home. Today I walk home. Tomorrow I will walk home.**).
	
	   e. Understand and use frequently occurring prepositions in English (e.g., *during, beyond, toward*).
	
	   f. Produce and expand complete declarative, interrogative, imperative, and exclamatory sentences in response to questions and prompts.
	
	   g. Understand that, minimally, every sentence must be about something (the subject) and tell something (the predicate) about its subject.

2. Observe conventions of capitalization, punctuation, and spelling.
 	
   a. Capitalize the first word in a sentence and the pronoun *I*.
 	
   b. Name and identify end punctuation, including periods, question marks, and exclamation points.
 	
   c. Spell simple words phonetically using knowledge of sound-letter relationships.
	2. Observe conventions of capitalization, punctuation, and spelling.
	
	   a. Capitalize names, places, and dates.
	
	   b. Use end punctuation for sentences, including periods, question marks, and exclamation points.
	
	   c. Use commas in dates and to separate single words in a series.
	
	   d. Use conventional spelling for words with common spelling patterns and for common irregular words.
	
	   e. Use phonetic spellings for untaught words, drawing on phonemic awareness and spelling conventions.
	
	   f. Form new words through addition, deletion, and substitution of sounds and letters (e.g., **an → man → mat → mast → must → rust → crust**).

Vocabulary Acquisition and Use

3. Determine word meanings (based on kindergarten reading).
 	
   a. Sort common objects into categories (e.g., shapes, foods) to gain a sense of the concepts the categories represent.
 	
   b. Identify new meanings for familiar words and apply them accurately (e.g., knowing **duck** as a bird and learning the verb to **duck**).
 	
   c. Use the most common affixes in English (e.g., **-ed, -s, re-, un-, pre-, -ful, -less**) as a clue to the meaning of an unknown word.
	3. Determine word meanings (based on grade 1 reading).
	
	   a. Sort words into categories (e.g., colors, clothing) to gain a sense of the concepts the categories represent.
	
	   b. Use sentence-level context as a clue to the meaning of an unknown word.
	
	   c. Use common affixes in English as a clue to the meaning of an unknown word.
	
	   d. Define words by category and by one or more key attributes (e.g., a **duck** is a bird that swims; a **tiger** is a large cat with stripes).
	
	   e. Demonstrate understanding of the concept of multiple-meaning words (e.g., **match, kind, play**) by identifying meanings of some grade-appropriate examples of such words.

(continued)

4. Understand word relationships.
 	
  a. Build real-life connections between words and their use (e.g., note places at school that are **colorful**).
 	
  b. Distinguish shades of meaning among verbs describing the same general action (e.g., **walk**, **march**, **strut**, **prance**) by acting out the meanings.
 	
  c. Use common adjectives to distinguish objects (e.g., the **small blue** square; the **shy white** rabbit).
 	
  d. Demonstrate understanding of common verbs and adjectives by relating them to their opposites (antonyms).
	4. Understand word relationships.
	
	  a. Build real-life connections between words and their use (e.g., note places at home that are **cozy**).
	
	  b. Distinguish shades of meaning among verbs differing in manner (e.g., **look, peek, glance, stare, glare, scowl**) and adjectives differing in intensity (e.g., **large, gigantic**) by defining, choosing, or acting out the meanings.

5. Use newly learned words acquired through conversations, reading, and responding to texts.	5. Use newly learned words acquired through conversations, reading, and responding to texts.

Grade 2 Students	Grade 3 Students
Conventions in Writing and Speaking	

1. Observe conventions of grammar and usage.
 	
  a. Form common irregular plural nouns (e.g., **feet, children, teeth, mice, fish**).
 	
  b. Form the past tense of common irregular verbs (e.g., **sat, hid, told**).
 	
  c. Produce and expand complete declarative, interrogative, imperative, and exclamatory sentences.
 	
  d. Produce and expand complete sentences to provide requested detail or clarification.
	1. Observe conventions of grammar and usage.
	
	  a. Explain the functions of nouns, pronouns, verbs, adjectives, and adverbs in general and their functions in specific sentences.
	
	  b. Form and use the simple verb tenses (e.g., **I walked. I walk. I will walk.**).
	
	  c. Ensure subject-verb and pronoun-antecedent agreement.
	
	  d. Produce simple, compound, and complex sentences.

2. Observe conventions of capitalization, punctuation, and spelling.
 	
  a. Capitalize holidays, product names, geographic names, and important words in titles.
 	
  b. Use commas in greetings and closings of letters.
 	
  c. Use apostrophes to form contractions and common possessives.
 	
  d. Generalize learned spelling patterns when writing words (e.g., **cage → badge; boy → boil; paper → copper**).
 	
  e. Consult reference materials, including beginning dictionaries, as needed to check and correct spellings.
	2. Observe conventions of capitalization, punctuation, and spelling.
	
	  a. Use correct capitalization.
	
	  b. Use quotation marks in dialogue.
	
	  c. Use conventional spelling for high-frequency and other studied words, and for adding suffixes to base words (e.g., **sitting, smiled, cries, happiness**).
	
	  d. Use spelling patterns and generalizations (e.g., word families, position-based spellings, syllable patterns, ending rules, meaningful word parts) in writing words.
	
	  e. Consult reference materials, including dictionaries, as needed to check and correct spellings.

	3. Make effective language choices. a. Use words for effect.

(continued)

Vocabulary Acquisition and Use	

4. Determine word meanings (based on grade 2 reading).
 	
  a. Determine or clarify the meaning of unknown or multiple-meaning words through the use of one or more strategies, such as understanding how the word is used in a sentence; analyzing the word's sounds, spelling, and meaningful parts; and consulting glossaries or beginning dictionaries, both print and digital.
 	
  b. Explain the meaning of grade-appropriate compound words (e.g., **birdhouse, lighthouse, housefly; bookshelf, notebook, bookmark**).
 	
  c. Use a known root word as a clue to the meaning of an unknown word with the same root (e.g., **addition, additional**).
 	
  d. Determine the meaning of the new word formed when a known prefix is added to a known word (e.g., **happy → unhappy, tell → retell**).
	4. Determine word meanings (based on grade 3 reading).
	
	  a. Determine or clarify the meaning of unknown or multiple-meaning words through the use of one or more strategies, such as understanding how the word is used in a sentence; analyzing the word's sounds, spelling, and meaningful parts; and consulting glossaries or beginning dictionaries, both print and digital.
	
	  b. Use a known root word as a clue to the meaning of an unknown word with the same root (e.g., **company, companion**).
	
	  c. Determine the meaning of the new word formed when a known affix is added to a known word (e.g., **agreeable → disagreeable, comfortable → uncomfortable, care → careless, heat → preheat**).
	
	  d. Distinguish the literal and non-literal meanings of words and phrases in context (e.g., **take steps**).

5. Understand word relationships.
 	
  a. Build real-life connections between words and their use (e.g., describe foods that are **spicy** or **juicy**).
 	
  b. Distinguish shades of meaning among related verbs (e.g., **toss, throw, hurl**) and related adjectives (e.g., **thin, slender, skinny, scrawny**).
	5. Understand word relationships.
	
	  a. Build real-life connections between words and their use (e.g., describe people who are **friendly** or **helpful**).
	
	  b. Distinguish among related words that describe states of mind or degrees of certainty (e.g., **knew, believed, suspected, heard, wondered**).

6. Use newly learned words acquired through conversations, reading, and responding to texts.	6. Use words that are common in conversational vocabulary as well as grade-appropriate academic vocabulary and domain-specific words (in English language arts, history/social studies, and science) taught directly and acquired through reading and responding to texts.

Appendix C
Spelling by Pattern, Level 2, Lesson 12

Lesson 12 The Goal Is to Know About <u>Long o</u>

<u>Long **o**</u> Can be Spelled <u>**oa**</u> or <u>**ow**</u>

Pattern Words

1. throw
2. throat
3. coast
4. yellow
5. toasted
6. soap
7. soaked
8. toad
9. snowed
10. window
11. shadow
12. growth
13. floating
14. coach
15. croak

Checklist

☐ Read the Pattern Words fast.

☐ Box the letters that spell the <u>long **o**</u> sound.

Happy Endings

• Write the Pattern Words with an ending after the main word.

Example: main word + ending = **sail** + **ed**

1. _____ + _____   2. _____ + _____

3. _____ + _____   4. _____ + _____

• Circle the word that is in present time.

Digraphs

Which two Pattern Words end with a digraph?

_____ and _____

Do You Know?

How is <u>long **o**</u> usually spelled at the end of a main word?

Circle one: **oa**   or   **ow**

Heart Words

16. would
17. could
18. should

1. Write the part of each heart word that is spelled the same.

   _____ _____ _____ _____

2. Which heart word begins with a digraph? _____

3. Which letter is silent in each heart word? _____

4. How is the vowel sound spelled in each heart word? _____

5. Which heart word sounds exactly like **wood**? _____

LETRS® Module 9, 2nd Edition

The Spell of Sound

ow and oa Practice

- Read these <u>long **o**</u> Pattern Words with endings.
- Box the spelling of the <u>long **o**</u> sound in the main word.
- Underline the endings of the other three words.

1.	t[o]a s t	t o a s t<u>e r</u>	t o a s t<u>e d</u>	t o a s t<u>i n g</u>
2.	s n o w	s n o w y	s n o w e d	s n o w i n g
3.	f l o a t	f l o a t e r	f l o a t e d	f l o a t i n g
4.	s o a k	s o a k s	s o a k e d	s o a k i n g
5.	c r o a k	c r o a k s	c r o a k e d	c r o a k i n g
6.	c o a c h	c o a c h e s	c o a c h e d	c o a c h i n g

- Read these <u>long **o**</u> words that are not on this lesson's word list.
- Continue to box and underline the word parts as above.

7.	s l o w	s l o w e r	s l o w e s t	s l o w l y
8.	o w n	o w n e r	o w n e d	o w n i n g
9.	l o a d	l o a d s	l o a d e d	l o a d i n g
10.	g r o a n	g r o a n s	g r o a n e d	g r o a n i n g
11.	r o a m	r o a m s	r o a m e d	r o a m i n g
12.	s h o w	s h o w s	s h o w y	s h o w e d

You can read harder <u>long **o**</u> words by dividing them into syllables.

- Can you read these words fast?
- First, underline the vowels.
- Next, divide the words between the middle consonant letters.
- Finally, box the syllable chunks.

1. 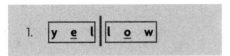   y e l l o w

2. a r r o w

3. p i l l o w

4. f e l l o w

5. w i n d o w

6. s h a l l o w

7. n a r r o w

8. e l b o w

9. h o l l o w

Extra for Experts!

Box the 3 syllable chunks in this word: | t o m o r r o w |

Primary Spelling by Pattern Level 2 Student

LETRS® Module 9, 2nd Edition

Word Hunt

Finding Words With the Right Meaning

Match one of these Pattern Words with the underline{long **o**} sound with each sentence.

throw	throat	coast	yellow	toasted
soap	soaked	toad	snowed	window
shadow	growth	floating	coach	croak

1. A _____ is an animal that looks like a frog but lives on land.

2. You're _____ when you are on top of the water and don't sink.

3. The color of lemons, bananas, and butter is _____.

4. To _____ means "to toss something into the air."

5. After it _____, we went sledding.

6. A _____ follows you around in the bright sunlight.

7. The sea meets the land along the _____.

8. A _____ is the sound that a frog makes.

9. You use _____ to get the dirt off your hands.

10. A _____ is made of glass and you can see through it.

11. The front of the neck is called the _____.

12. We _____ marshmallows by the fireside.

13. A great _____ makes good players better.

14. It rained so hard we got _____.

15. The _____ of a puppy is faster than that of a baby.

Heart Work

Heart words do not look the way they sound!

would	could	should

Heart Word Contractions

An apostrophe always takes the place of one or more letters.

would + **not** = wouldn**ot** = **wouldn't**

could + **not** = couldn**ot** = **couldn't**

should + **not** = shouldn**ot** = **shouldn't**

Heart Word Sentences

Choose the right form of this lesson's heart words to write in the blanks.

1. **could** or **couldn't**

    They said it _____ be done, but I did it!

2. **would** or **wouldn't**

    I _____ ride a bike without a helmet if I were you.

3. **should** or **shouldn't**

    You _____ use good language when you speak.

4. **would** or **wouldn't**

    I _____ go to school if I were not so sick.

5. **should** or **shouldn't**

    You _____ talk with food in your mouth.

6. **could** or **couldn't**

    I _____ check out a book if I went to the library.

The middle of these heart words is **OUL = Oh, You Elle!**

I Can Do It!

Can You Write It?

- Read these sentences.
- Circle all the words that have the <u>long **o**</u> spelled **oa** or **ow**.
- Be ready to write these sentences when they are read to you.

1. Our drive was slow because of snow on the road.

2. The toad jumped in the window and began to croak.

3. Some soap was floating while I was soaking in the tub.

4. Our throats were scratchy after we got soaked in the yellow boat.

5. Did you throw my toast to the crows?

- How many words did you find with **oa**? _____

- How many words did you find with **ow**? _____

Can You Fix It?

- Box the words that are spelled wrong.
- Write the sentence, fixing all of the mistakes, including capital letters and punctuation.

1. the yelow towd croakt when it saw its shadoaw

   _____

   _____

   _____

2. we went to the koast to flote and soke in the soapy sea suds

   _____

   _____

   _____

3. our coch told us we showd growth in throing balls

   _____

   _____

   _____

On Safari
Safari Journal: "High-Low, the Giraffe"

Our safari guide tells us another story. He says that a giraffe with a sore throat must be a very sad thing, but this story has a happy ending.

- Circle all of the Pattern Words in this lesson you can find.

High-Low, the giraffe, lived in a tree house on the coast of the sea. She liked to look out the window and watch the boats.

One day she saw a yellow box floating by. It had big letters on it that spelled "soap." She got soaked when she swam out to get it. It had snowed the day before. It was cold there in the shadow of the tree house. She could feel her throat getting sore, but she just had to get the box.

She got a big surprise. Inside the box was a toad! He smiled and let out a big croak. High-Low thought he might be a rich prince with a golden coach. She gave him a kiss. He did not turn into a prince. The toad just laughed and said, "Let's throw a log on the fire and have toasted marshmallows."

She got well, and the growth of their friendship never slowed down.

Reading Fluency (157 Words)
How long does it take you to read "High-Low, the Giraffe"? _____

Word Sort and Rapid-Reading Flash Cards

Follow the directions on the *Lesson 12 Word Sort* sheet your teacher has given you.

Primary Spelling by Pattern Level 2 Student

Appendix D
A Home for Lizzie

by Beth Thompson

I was in the backyard pretending I was a goldminer and searching for treasure when I saw Lizzie. She was sitting on a rock, not moving at all. She could have been a leaf or a twig, because her nubbly skin blended in with the dark grey stone. But she was watching me. Then slowly blinked her shiny, black eyes. It was like saying hello.

I named her Lizzie. When I said her name out loud, she lifted herself up on her tiny toes as if she were going to tiptoe away. But she didn't go. I guess she liked her name.

I think Lizzie knew I didn't want to hurt her. When I touched her back, she twitched her long, skinny tail. Maybe she thought my finger was a strange, new, bug!

The sun had warmed Lizzie's rock. Now the rock felt like the back steps under bare toes. "Does that feel good to your toes, too?" I asked her. But Lizzie only blinked a blink that could mean "yes" . . . or could mean "no." And I don't know lizard language.

I found an empty butter tub under the kitchen sink. It was smooth and white and just the right size for a lizard home. It had a plastic almost-see-through lid. Mom helped me punch holes in the lid. I made six holes, so Lizzie would get lots of air.

I picked a handful of grass and sprinkled it inside the tub. Then I showed it to Lizzie.

"Look, your very own room," I told her. "You don't have to share." She blinked. " It has air conditioning. And a nice green rug you can nibble on. Do you like it?" Lizzie blinked "yes" . . . but it might have been "no."

I set her carefully on the grass in the tub. Then I put on the lid. I peeked through the holes to see what she would do.

Lizzie didn't move at first. Then she tried to climb up the side of the butter tub, but it was too smooth. She slid back to the grass and sat very still. She couldn't hide against the white plastic or the green grass. She couldn't warm herself against the cold, smooth tub. She couldn't feel the sun through the plastic ceiling of her new home.

I took off the lid and held it over my head, pretending I was Lizzie. Six tiny bits of sun shone through a cloudy window that needed washing. The wilted grass felt limp and coarse. Then I sniffed the tub. It smelled like butter and plastic and soap-under-the-sink, not at all like the backyard.

So I took Lizzie out of the butter tub and put her back on the rock. She didn't make a sound or run away. She just sat there, blinking. But I knew this time she meant "yes," because now Lizzie was home.

Answer Key

Chapter 1
The Challenge of Learning to Write

Exercise 1.1: List the Benefits of Writing (p. 7)
   (No Answer Key. Responses will vary.)

Exercise 1.2: Compare Kindergarten and First-Grade Writing Samples (p. 11)

Question	Kindergarten Student	First-Grade Student
Has the student automatized standard letter formation?	**Yes. Printing is controlled, well-formed, and between the lines.**	**No. Letters are formed poorly and with apparent effort. Spacing is not controlled. Thus, the student has written less.**
Does the student need more work on the use of uppercase and lowercase letters?	**Lowercase letter formation is established. The student needs some practice with formation of uppercase letters and decisions about when to use them.**	**The student confuses uppercase and lowercase; appears to have "invented" the order and direction of strokes.**
Does the student have control over spaces and the alignment of writing on the page?	**Yes.**	**No. Spacing is either too spread out or too cramped.**

Does the student represent the sounds in words (demonstrating grade-appropriate phoneme awareness)?	Yes. Words such as "sleve," "shrt," and "micee mouse" represent all of the sounds, even though the student doesn't yet know the standard spelling.	Yes. "Mad him get frins," for example, is pretty good phonetic spelling.
Does the student have grade-appropriate command of high-frequency irregular word spellings (orthographic memory)?	Yes, the student has advanced knowledge for grade level; *there*, *get*, *when*, *will go*, and *to* are all correct.	The student has *was*, *a*, *he*, *in*, *have*, and *they*—but is guessing at *get*, *any*, and *made*. This skill level is not great for the end of first grade.
Does the student use punctuation appropriately (orthographic and syntactic knowledge)?	The student is mostly successful at marking stops at the end of statements.	The student doesn't use any punctuation.
Do you think the student was positively engaged by the task?	Yes, because of the length of the composition, adherence to the topic, and the level of detail supplied.	No; the "word bank" is unused. The student may not have understood the assignment. He/she wrote a story instead of a description.

Now, write a short paragraph (three to five sentences) that compares these two students' development of phonological, orthographic, and graphomotor skills in relation to the overall quality of their compositions. **Although they're a grade apart, the students are notably different in their skill levels. The kindergarten student has mastered letter formation, spelling of high-frequency irregular words, phonetic spelling of unknown words, and left to right spacing. The kindergarten student is better able to write a coherent narrative and transcribe words onto the page than is the first-grader, whose story is constrained by poorly established letter formation and transcription skills.**

Exercise 1.3: List Higher-Level and Lower-Level Cognitive Demands (p. 16)

Higher-Level Cognitive Demands	Lower-Level Cognitive Skills
1. Using a story structure or expository structure.	1. Physically forming the letters using pencil on paper.
2. Varying sentence structure.	2. Writing left to right.
3. Sticking to the plan.	3. Spacing words on the page.
4. Using topic sentences in paragraphs.	4. Spelling high-frequency irregular words.
5. Keeping the goal of the composition in mind.	5. Phonetically spelling unknown words.
6. Keeping the audience's needs in mind.	6. Using uppercase letters as appropriate.
7. Checking for insufficient or unnecessary detail.	7. Using end punctuation.
8. Choosing precise vocabulary to express ideas.	8. Indenting paragraphs.

Exercise 1.4: Evaluate Three Second-Grade Students (p. 18)

Three second-graders (none receiving special education services) were asked at the end of the academic year to write a description of how they would make breakfast for a friend. After a few minutes of discussion of the topic, they had 20 minutes to write. Look over the three writing samples, then answer each question below in a single sentence.

Translations:

1. I went in to the kitchen and make chocolate chip waffles for Tyonnie and me, Siera. I put the waffle in the toaster. I let it sit for 15 minutes. Once it's finished, we eat it.

2. I make cereal for me. I fix my own cereal. Then I eat my cereal. It was good. I do it every day. I make cereal for my friend. He likes cereal, too. My friend is nice to me. I'm nice to him, too.

3. I like to make cereal. First, you get the milk and cereal and bowl and spoon, then pour the cereal and milk, then you eat it.

Questions:

1. Which two students exhibit the least accurate phonetic representations in their spelling? Citing specific errors, defend your opinion about which students need additional work on phonological awareness and basic phoneme-grapheme correspondence.

   Student #1 and Student #3 have some markedly inaccurate phonological representations in their spelling. In the first writing sample, the words *kitchen*, *chocolate*, *waffle*, and *finished* are missing sounds or have misplaced sounds. In the third writing sample, the spellings for *cereal* and *milk* show underdeveloped phoneme identification and sequencing abilities. Until students can represent the sounds and their sequences fairly accurately, they should continue to work on word pronunciation, phoneme segmentation, phoneme-grapheme mapping, and encoding. Without solid foundations in these areas, students will try to rely on rote visual memory to spell—and that is not a productive strategy.

2. Why do you think the sentences are so short in writing sample #2?

   Several possibilities might explain the brevity of Bradie's sentences and sparseness of verbal expression. First, his verbal expressive language skills and vocabulary, in spoken language, might be underdeveloped. Second, he seems highly conscious of writing a "complete sentence" because he uses a standard, simple sentence form with a capital letter and a period at the end. Third, he might be disinterested in the topic, because he first wrote about his own breakfast and only discussed his friend at the end of the piece.

3. What is your best guess about the nature, quality, and amount of writing instruction these students have received?

   In the classrooms from which these samples were drawn, observational data documented that, on average, only 6 percent of instructional time involved any kind of writing instruction, and in one-third of the classrooms, there was no instruction in writing at all. High-quality instruction occurred in only a small proportion of observed classes across 17 elementary schools (Moats, Foorman, & Taylor, 2006).

Exercise 1.5: Observe Working Memory at Work (p. 24)

Read the compositions of two additional second-grade students, who were also asked to write a description of how they would make breakfast for a friend. Then, discuss with a partner how the writing samples differ. What can "T." do that Jasmine has not yet mastered? Could memory processes play a role in these differences?

T.'s composition is more integrated than Jasmine's. Jasmine writes her ideas in a list. Her thinking and sequencing of ideas are organized, but she does not yet have the ability to hold her ideas in mind while she writes sentences that are connected to one another in a narrative flow. T., in contrast, can hold the image of the event in mind while connecting one idea to the next in longer sentences with descriptive detail.

Chapter 2
Teaching Handwriting and Spelling

Exercise 2.3: Identify Spelling Errors in Students' Writing (p. 41)

The following sentences were lifted from second-graders' written work. Each sentence contains one or more misspelled words. Can you identify a specific spelling concept that each student needs to learn?

1. I'm *gowing* to make breakfast for my friend.
   /ō/ is a rounded back vowel. The /w/ sound is not spelled in this word. This student needs to learn the spelling of the base word, go.

2. I will put it on a *plaet* (**plate**).
   This student needs to learn the long-vowel spelling convention VCe.

3. I will sit *donw* and eat.
   ow spells /ou/ in down.

4. I will cook *pancake*.
   The inflection /s/ must be spelled.

5. *Frist, yous* (**use**) eggs.
   Vowel-r combinations are welded sounds; the vowel letter always comes before the /r/, as in first. For the word use, the student should learn that the /yu/ sound is often spelled with the letter u, and the word use is a VCe pattern.

6. I'm going to have a *chawBaer* (**strawberry**).
   The /t/ before /r/ in strawberry is affricated in pronunciation and sounds like /ch/. The mouth is fooling us with tr and str blends.

7. We made *froot silit* (**fruit salad**). You need *grabes* and *strawberrys* and *watermelem*.
   This student needs more instruction at the level of phoneme identification and sequencing. The student uses two consonant voicing substitutions (silit/salad; grabes/grapes) and a nasal confusion of /m/ for /n/ in watermelon.

8. You can make pancakes with *agg* and with *mike* (**egg** and **milk**).
   The first sound in egg is actually like /ā/; the mouth is fooling us. The tongue is raised up to say /g/ and distorts the vowel sound. But this students needs to listen for the l- blend in milk.

9. I like to make *breakthis*.
   This fricative substitution—/th/ for /f/—and omission of the final /t/ suggest that this student needs more work on pronunciation, phoneme segmentation, and phoneme differentiation.

10. Then the *yok* (**yolk**) comes out of the egg.

    This is an orthographic error: right sounds, wrong symbols. Needs the silent -lk spelling pattern.

11. I *craked* it; then the slime came out.

    The student needs to learn the –ck rule: Use –ck for /k/ right after a short vowel.

Chapter 3
Sentences

Exercise 3.1: Brush Up on Labels for Word Functions (p. 45)

Below is a short passage. Can you identify the role that each word is playing in the sentence frame? Label the role of each word, using the code in *Table 3.1*.

c   det. adj.   n.   v.   prep. prep. pn adj.   n.   det. n.   c.   cop.
Then the Yellow Corn-Maiden brought from under her torn blanket a pouch, [which was]

v.   prep. n.   c.   adv.   v.   prep.   n.   c. det. adj.   n.
made of buckskin and artfully beaded with turquoise and the whitest shells.

Exercise 3.2: Classify Types of Phrases (p. 49)

Next to each phrase, note which of three syntactic categories the phrase belongs to: noun phrase (NP), verb phrase (VP), or prepositional phrase (PP).

after the concert __PP__   the bitter cold winter __NP__   fluctuated daily __VP__

sold reluctantly __VP__   any golden variety __NP__   fed regularly __VP__

without a thought __PP__   over the top __PP__   deep knowledge __NP__

a chance encounter __NP__   was trekking __VP__   under the table __PP__

Exercise 3.3: Differentiate Between Phrases and Clauses (p. 50)

Sort the following phrases and clauses into the appropriate column in the chart.

Phrase	Independent Clause	Dependent Clause
before twilight	Perry called	whenever we go camping
the tangled roots	we dined out last Friday	where Italian is spoken
spectacular fine dining	the symphony concluded	because he loves chocolate waffles
driven to distraction	visiting can be tiresome	after the performance ended

Exercise 3.4: Identify Simple, Compound, and Complex Sentences (p. 52)

Write "**S**" for simple, "**CP**" for compound, or "**CX**" for complex next to each sentence below.

__CX__ She was an old woman who lived at the bottom of the hill.

__S__ The Incas built a city high in the Andes.

__CX__ The skin of poisonous frogs keeps predators away because it tastes bitter.

__CP__ Winter days are short, so we play more indoor sports in that season.

__S__ Egyptian mummies were buried inside the pyramids.

__CP__ The dog barked incessantly, but the owners did nothing to stop it.

__CX__ Whenever the control tower gives the signal, the plane takes off.

__S__ Carlos, the forward, sank the winning basket in overtime.

__CP__ The odds were in her favor, yet she still placed second.

__CX__ Whenever we are available, he is willing to guide us.

Chapter 4
Supporting the Planning Process

Exercise 4.1: Practice Listing (p. 76)
(No Answer Key. Responses will vary.)

Exercise 4.2: Select Writing Assignment Prompts and Cues (p. 77)

The Banjo Lesson, Henry O. Tanner—This informal portrait depicts an affectionate, patient father or grandfather teaching his boy how to play the banjo. It could be used to prompt a personal narrative about learning something new; a description of the relationship between the characters; or a persuasive piece about why we love/need music in our lives. Questions: *Have you ever tried to play an instrument? Who is teaching you? Do you like music? What kind? When do you listen to music? What is your favorite song/band/singer? Why do you think this boy is learning from his father/grandfather?*

Snap the Whip, Winslow Homer—This game is probably known to almost all kids; all it requires is a long enough line of players. It can be played on ice skates and telemark skis, too. It can prompt the writing of a sequence or explanation: "How to Play Crack the Whip." The transition words first, then, next, and finally are a good fit for describing how to play this game. Personal experience might come into play, as some students love being on the end of the "whip" while others fear it.

The Gulf Stream, Winslow Homer—Of all the paintings in our collection, this is the most provocative. The man on the boat could be rescued by the ship—or maybe not. He might be coming out of a storm—or going into one. He might die—or he might live, overcoming the dangers. This picture is a great stimulus for story-telling. *Who is this man? Where did he come from? Where was he trying to go? How did his boat get wrecked? Will he escape the sharks, waves, and wind and be rescued?*

A Basket of Clams, Winslow Homer—This picture can be used to encourage inferences about time, place, smell, touch, and activity. Some background information about clams would be important. Clams live about 8–12 inches below the sand's surface near the edge of a calm, salt water bay or inlet. They are dug up with a trowel, often at low tide. Clam-diggers can find them by watching for their air bubbles. *Where are these boys? Is the sun shining? Are they near the water? How does it smell right there? What do they feel on their feet? Why would they be digging clams? Why might that boat be up on the sand? Would you like to dig for clams? Do you like to eat them?*

The Wedding Feast, Pieter Bruegel—Old as the scene is, it also has timeless appeal. There are many features that invite description. Questions to ask include: *What is the occasion?* (A party, a wedding celebration.) *Who is getting married?* (The girl in front of the green backdrop.) *What is the mood of this crowd?* (Joyous.) *How do you know?* (Musicians; feasting; sharing; talking; drinking.) *Why would the artist put the food tray and the drinking pitcher right in the front of the painting?* (So we are drawn right into the action, ready for our share!) *Are children in the picture? What are they doing?* (They are included in the feast and allowed to be comfortable and eat with their fingers.) More advanced: *Why would the bride have her hands folded and her eyes closed, while everyone else is talking, drinking, or eating? Do you think these are (materially) rich people or poor people? Why? Peacock feathers symbolize or stand for balance, harmony, and good health. Why would the painter put one in the foreground of this picture?*

Rocky Mountains, Lander's Peak, Albert Bierstadt—Although the painter purposefully exaggerated the size and grandeur of the mountain peak, to impress Easterners who had never been to the Wild West, he also portrayed in great detail the domestic life of a Plains Indian tribe. This painting could prompt a description of the scene, possibly from the point of view of an Indian child. Where would you sleep if you were an Indian child? What animals would you take care of? What would you eat? What chores would you have? Would you like being in this valley? What would be the advantages? The disadvantages?

Creole Women of Color Out Taking the Air, Édouard Marquis—This image could prompt a description or a narrative. The women are proud, self-conscious, young, saucy, and ready for some important event. *Where are the women going? Why are they dressed up? Are they friends? Sisters? Can you think of what might happen next? Does one of them catch your attention in particular? Why?*

Exercise 4.3: Collaborate to Determine a Purpose for Student Writing (p. 82)

(No Answer Key. Responses will vary.)

Exercise 4.4: Evaluate a Student Writing Sample, Third Grade (p. 85)

What do you think happened to this third-grade student as he was writing his personal narrative about his "perfect weekend"? What could his teacher have done to help him improve the cohesion and focus of this piece?
The student lost focus midstream. He could not keep the goal and topic in mind, and it is unclear whether either of these was established before he began writing. Students like this can benefit from considerable preparation, including talking through what the written piece will say; adopting a visual framework that specifies the topic and details before writing begins; and coaching the students to ask themselves, "Am I saying what I said I would say?"

Chapter 5
Enabling Translation

Warm-Up: Putting Ideas Into Words

Have you ever known a student who seemed to "know a lot" but couldn't come up with the words to express himself or herself? Brainstorm at least five possible causes for this behavior.

1. **Limited practice formulating ideas into words.**

2. **Lack of modeling or encouragement to speak at home or in school.**

3. **Limited vocabulary, impoverished word store.**

4. **Word retrieval difficulties (words are there but can't be accessed).**

5. **English language learner with limited language proficiency.**

6. **Developmental language disorder that encompasses syntactic formulation and retrieval.**

Exercise 5.1: Evaluate First-Grade Writing Samples (p. 90)

Student #1, C.P. Composition in grade 1, early January.
Reading and writing are closely connected, as illustrated by these three cases. The student who is above-benchmark in reading decoding, fluency, and comprehension can write a lengthy composition. His sentences are long and varied, and he deliberately tries to connect the ideas. He concludes his narrative with a summary statement.

Student #2, N.C. Composition in grade 1, early December.
The second student is in a later phonetic stage of spelling, mildly delayed for grade level. She has learned, through intervention, to write the sounds in words and has started to automatize spellings for high-frequency vocabulary. She is not yet able to choose interesting words or vary her sentence structure, but we can read and understand the message.

Student #3, J.D.: Composition in grade 1, January.

The third student, who is at risk and well below benchmark on screening, is still working on mastery of the alphabetic principle. He can represent a few sounds with letters, but he has written no complete or even decipherable words. Letter formation habits are not yet established. Since early spelling depends on phoneme awareness, his severe deficit in this area needs to be addressed before he can make much progress with the transcription of written language.

Chapter 6
Review, Revision, and Publication

Exercise 6.1: Give Corrective Feedback (p. 98)
Answers will vary, but should include such comments as:

- Look at the spelling of **use**. Say the first sound. What letters can represent that sound, /y/?
- This sentence needs a capital letter somewhere. Can someone tell me where it goes, and why it goes there?
- This sentence needs a punctuation mark at the end. Which one should it be? Why?
- These sentences were written together. Is there any way we can combine the ideas in these two sentences? Does the first sentence say when we can use the father's workbench? What can you add that tells when this can happen?

Exercise 6.3: Plan a Writing Lesson (p. 104)
(No Answer Key. Responses will vary.)

Index

Note: Page numbers in *italics* refer to the Answer Key.

W